A MILLION PROSECUTOR MISTAKES

How They Lost the Trial

of Trayvon Martin's Confessed Killer

(George Zimmerman)

HONEY HOWARD ROTHSCHILD
Attorney at Law and Prosecutor

A MILLION PROSECUTOR MISTAKES:
How They Lost the Trial of Trayvon Martin's Confessed Killer
(George Zimmerman)

ISBN: 978-1-7347286-0-6 (hardcover)
ISBN: 979-86511-39-996 (paperback)
ISBN: 978-1-7347286-2-0 (ebook)
Library of Congress Catalog Control Number (LCCN) 2020904187
eab:20200325

PUBLISHED BY:
R.E.S.T.O.R.E Community Justice, Inc. 30628 Detroit Rd No. 194
Cleveland, OH 44145

William Shakespeare Henry VI, Part 2, Act IV, Scene 2:

"The first thing we do, let's kill all the lawyers"

In the 1500's when Shakespeare wrote his poems and plays, criminals conspired to destroy England's social order and stability. Although the quote appears to suggest that killing the lawyers would save society, the statement was made by a character in the play who was a murderer and an anarchist. He plotted to get rid of the lawyers and destroy enforcement of the laws.

CONTENTS

DEDICATION

TO TRAYVON MARTIN

"An American Tragedy: Trayvon Martin's Death," was on the cover of the April 15, 2012 issue of *People* magazine. As I read the article about your senseless killing, tears stung at the back of my eyes. You were only 17 years old! You could have invented a flying bicycle or found a cure for cancer.

Instead, your potential was taken away from you, your family and the world forever.

Determined that I would never forget what happened to you, I placed the magazine in the center of my living room table. I promised to watch the trial of your killer and see that you got justice. And when the prosecutors failed to convict George Zimmerman (referred to as "GZ" in this book), I was outraged. Because the volunteer neighborhood watchman had confessed at the scene, putting him in prison should have been easy. I know, because I was a prosecutor for 30 years.

And so, I made you another promise. I vowed that I would write a book to expose the truth about what went wrong during that trial. And now, eight years later, here it is, *A Million Prosecutor Mistakes: How They Lost the Trial of Trayvon Martin's Confessed Killer (George Zimmerman)*. I'm very sorry that my book comes too late to get justice for you. However, because of your sacrifice, the families of future crime victims will know what prosecutors are supposed to do and use the information provided in this book to make sure they get justice for their loved ones.

Furthermore, this book can be used as a guide for groups and organizations that were founded in response to the acquittal of your killer to evaluate the performances of prosecutors and work with communities across the country to vote out the incompetent ones along with the bosses who appointed them.

TO TRAYVON MARTIN'S PARENTS

Losing a child this way is the most terrible thing that can happen to any parent. Adding to your pain is the fact that you were sent on a *Don Quixote* quest by Angela Corey's team of prosecutors to find out why your son's confessed killer was set free when it was all their fault due to their incompetence and lack of motivation to convict George Zimmerman (who is referred to as "GZ" in my book.)

Unfortunately, you can't sue prosecutors for malpractice. They represented the people of Florida and as a result, you have little recourse against them. Furthermore, the state's lawyer's oath that they took didn't require them to zealously represent the people. All Corey's team had to do was show up—which is precisely what they did when they prosecuted your son's killer. By contrast, lawyers in Ohio must swear to put forth our best efforts in every case or risk sanctions from the local bar associations and the Ohio Supreme Court, which set high standards for the practice of law.

Following GZ's acquittal, you asked President Barack Obama to go through the details of the shooting of your son with a fine-tooth comb.

While he couldn't risk a conflict of interest by interfering with the Department of Justice's investigation into the case, please know that I have done that for you. I recorded the trial and replayed it many times over and scrupulously examined all the evidence and testimony of the witnesses, both for the prosecution and the defense.

A Million Prosecutor Mistakes: How They Lost the Trial of Trayvon Martin's Confessed Killer (George Zimmerman) is the result of my six years of research and many sleepless nights. At last, in these pages you will find in plain talk, not lawyer mumbo jumbo, the answers to the question that wakes you up at night: Why did the prosecutors fail to hold Trayvon's confessed killer accountable for taking my son's life?

Special Prosecutor Angela Corey's team quickly turned what should have been an open and shut case into a losing hot mess. The crafty defense team exploited their weaknesses and made the prosecutors look like *The Three Stooges* pretending to be real lawyers.

After they blew it, the prosecutors claimed they had no clue what went wrong. And now, seven years later, they still refuse to accept full responsibility for their amateur performance during the trial. My hope is to dispel the misguided outrage against Florida's "Stand Your Ground" law and expose this small group of prosecutors for refusing to admit that it was their fault that Trayvon and your family didn't get justice.

TO GRANT BUTLER, MY FIRST EDITOR

Thank you, my dear friend, for your steady support and belief in me and the importance of this book project.

TO MY PARENTS JUDGE JOHN AND GLADYS HOWARD

I find comfort in knowing that you are still guiding my steps from Heaven. Thank you for everything. I love and miss you more than I can say.

FINALLY, I DEDICATE THIS BOOK TO EVERY AMERICAN

Never let anyone stop your search for the truth, the whole truth, and nothing but the truth!

Too many of my fellow prosecutors and lawyers have forgotten that this obligation also applies to us.

INTRO:

WHY I WROTE THIS BOOK

At quitting time, I often left my job at the U.S. Virgin Islands Attorney General's office to go for a dip in the shimmering turquoise sea, a block away. My body would be chilled from working all day in air conditioning and it felt so good when my toes sank into that warm white sand.

I would hurry behind a cluster of sea grapes where I stripped to the bikini under my clothes. Then I would run into the water and slide under the gentle waves where I would marvel at the multicolored fishes. When my lungs were out of air, I would surface and float awhile on my back.

One day, I was belly up basking in the hot sun when I became aware of someone swimming toward me. It was a West Indian man. Long and black, he flashed a fiendish white grin and rather reminded me of a shark.

"Remember me?" he demanded. But I didn't know him from Adam. "I'm sorry," I stammered.

His eyes blazed with anger. My head jerked toward the beach. It was deserted. My legs trembled as I tried to tread water, which I wasn't that good at even when I wasn't terrified. Instantly, I regretted picking this spot because it was so isolated. I realized there was no point in screaming for help. Tourists didn't come there and the locals who swam earlier in the day had all gone home.

"You sent me and my father to the joint!" the man bellowed.

Recognition dawned and I remembered him all too well. I was a prosecutor and he and his father were my first felony convictions for attempted murder for brutally pistol whipping a man.

I said to myself, so this is how it all ends? On a lonely beach in American paradise? All this felon had to do was push my head under and I was done – shark bait that no one would ever find, except, maybe, in tiny chunks.

Momma told me to never swim without a buddy. As my legs started cramping from the tension, I wished I had listened to her.

I agonized over what to do. Should I chicken out and claim mistaken identity? My moment of truth was at hand and the test of my character that people who prided themselves with high principles dreaded.

"As much as we all would like to take the law into our own hands," I heard myself saying boldly, "we can't go around trying to kill folks just because they pissed us off!"

The convict stared hard at me for a long moment. Then he broke into a grin. "I had a lot of time to think in the joint and…I know you were just doing your job."

Relief swept over my body and I went limp. As I sank toward the bottom of the ocean, he pulled me up to the surface. The man I had sent to prison paddled back to shore, cradling me gently in his strong grip while he explained how he found Jesus in prison. Praise the Lord!

Now, you may ask, what does my story about this felon have to do with the prosecutors of Trayvon Martin's killer? Everything! In the summer of 2013 when defense lawyer Mark O'Mara and his sidekick Don West soundly defeated their efforts to convict George Zimmerman (hereinafter referred to as "GZ"), Angela Corey's team failed their own test of character by refusing to admit they deserved an "F" for how they had conducted the trial.

To say they made a million mistakes is an exaggeration. However, the prosecutors made so many errors I couldn't count them all. Almost every time Bernie De La Rionda, John Guy, and Richard Mantei opened their mouths, they got the facts, the law, or the rules of criminal procedure and evidence all wrong.

While they put on a show, the lack of a winning strategy caused them to work harder than necessary. Too often they were clueless and got stuck in areas they never should have opened up in the first place.

The defense team, Mark O'Mara and Don West must still be laughing at how easily they defeated these prosecutors. Delighted to exploit their mistakes, they continually sidetracked the jury from the central issue of whether GZ had killed Trayvon in self-defense or whether he had shot him with a depraved indifference to human life.

At the end of the trial, the teenager's killer sped in his pick-up truck down a dusty road in Texas. Tucked in his glove box was the 9 mm Kel-Tec murder weapon. Meanwhile, Special Prosecutor Angela Corey and her team went on television and denied responsibility for GZ's acquittal! Claiming they did their best, De La Rionda, the lead prosecutor, clasped his hands and shrugged his shoulders. Smiling sheepishly, he claimed it was only the second time he had lost a criminal trial in his entire career.

Having watched the trial live and replayed it on my DVR several times, that was hard for me to believe. As explained with specific examples between the pages of my book, the GZ prosecutors deviated from standard trial tactics too often and made far too many mistakes.

Although every prosecutor knows there is no such thing as a perfect trial because something always goes wrong, it's usually something of little consequence like putting the wrong label on an exhibit. Rarely, is it a huge mistake like forgetting to contact a witness. While a few errors can be expected, covering them up is wrong. That's why the refusal of these four sworn officers of the court to admit they made any mistakes at all while losing what should have been an easy conviction provoked me to write this book and set the record straight.

A Million Prosecutor Mistakes: How They Lost the Trial of Trayvon Martin's Confessed Killer (George Zimmerman) contradicts and disproves the prosecutors' statements that they did their best and didn't know why they had lost the trial. No way! Over my 30-year career as a prosecutor, I have never seen so many errors in a single trial. Even if I added all the errors that my colleagues made to those I had read about, the total would not even come close to the staggering number of mistakes these prosecutors made during GZ's trial.

My book thoroughly examines the poor decisions, from John Guy's appalling opening statement to De La Rionda's lame closing arguments. An opening statement is the prosecutor's best chance to make a good impression on the jury. Instead, Guy opened the trial and disrespected the six women jurors with "Fucking punks! These assholes always get away!" Although it was a direct quote from GZ when he first spotted Trayvon Martin that fateful night, never break the cardinal rule, "Never curse at the jury."

As the trial progressed, these prosecutors acted like the Three Stooges. As their mistakes kept piling up, they made me wonder if they were trying to lose. A prime example, they failed to explain the motive to the jury why GZ had killed Trayvon Martin. They didn't take the time to be selective and called too many witnesses. Of the 38, only four were necessary to convict the volunteer neighborhood watchman of second-degree murder. It appeared that Corey's team didn't know how to force the killer to testify so they could tear his lies apart during cross-examination.

Furthermore, these prosecutors didn't ask their witnesses the right questions and they didn't know how to cross-examine the defense witnesses. Not even a first-year lawyer would have risked calling an unprepared witness, such as Rachel Jeantel, to prove crucial elements of their case when they didn't even speak her language. Why didn't these prosecutors consult with a linguist who could have helped them interpret her slang before they put her in front of the jury? They were clueless about what she was going to say and were caught off-guard when she testified that Trayvon had referred to as a "creepy ass cracker." That bombshell allowed the defense to put the victim on trial for being a racist.

At last, in plain, non-lawyer talk, my book lays out the countless mistakes Angela Corey's team made that allowed Trayvon Martin's killer to go free. All the blame belongs squarely on the shoulders of the prosecutors and I sincerely hope that exposing the truth will encourage them to finally admit they didn't put forth their best efforts. Instead, they continue to deny any responsibility.

But if they weren't to blame for Trayvon's killer getting off, who was?

During their television interviews, I had cringed watching the prosecutors whine and shift the blame for their loss onto the laws of Florida. And more disgusting, they implied it was Rachel Jeantel's fault. She was the love- struck teenager who never should have been called to testify in the first place.

Considering this team boasted 95 years of criminal trial experience among them, the time has long since passed for these prosecutors to do what they had always required of their witnesses and tell the truth, the whole truth, and nothing but the truth. They had misgivings about the case from the start because they were forced to go against the Sanford Police who didn't want to bring charges against GZ. When they let him go home, the public outcry and demands for justice pressured Florida Governor Scott to appoint a special prosecutor. Then Angela Corey charged the neighborhood vigilante with second-degree murder for killing the black teenager.

Since GZ had confessed at the scene, convicting him should have been easy. Instead, it was a farce and a gross miscarriage of justice.

Many people still want to know why these prosecutors failed to convict this guy who had strapped on a gun with lethal hollow point bullets and took the life of an unarmed teenager.

A more urgent concern of this author is that Trayvon Martin's parents were deceived. Knowing they were to blame, the prosecutors sent Sybrina Fulton and Tracy Martin on an impossible Don Quixote quest to find out why their son's killer was set free.

And now, it is my sincere hope that the analysis of GZ's second-degree murder case by me, an experienced prosecutor, provides in specific details the many ways the prosecutors failed to do their job and bring the desperately needed closure to Trayvon's parents who will, at last, find the answers to the questions that wake them up at night.

On December 3, 2019, the opportunity to finally get even more of the answers we all seek came from an unexpected source when GZ had the gall to file a civil lawsuit against Trayvon's parents, the prosecutors, and others from his trial. It's a blessing in disguise, because the killer has no right to remain silent in a civil lawsuit. Now that he can no longer hide the truth behind that privilege, the named defendants can take his deposition and those of the other witnesses the prosecutors failed to properly question.

Even better, a public records request can be made to get the documents from the Department of Justice's now-closed investigation into Trayvon's killing. An FBI profile and behavioral analysis of the killer that the prosecutors failed to request should be included. As a result, GZ's real motive may be discovered whether it was to retaliate against the black youth for the previous break-ins by other prowlers or the motive was to intimidate his wife Shellie, who had left him the night before the volunteer neighborhood watchman went on patrol and shot Trayvon on February 26, 2012.

Between 2002 and 2012, almost twice as many women were killed by their spouses (11,766) as there were casualties (6,488) in the Afghanistan and Iraq wars combined. On an average day, more than 20,000 phone calls are placed to domestic violence hotlines nationwide and three women are slain every day.

Beating and killing your partner has become an epidemic. And yet, Corey's team failed to connect the dots and uncover that intimidating his wife was GZ's most compelling motive for killing an unarmed teenager after stalking him.

1

KILLING TRAYVON MARTIN

SANFORD, FLORIDA:

Back in 1946, Sanford became infamous when Jackie Robinson, the first black player for a major league baseball team, the Brooklyn Dodgers, was chased out of town by a lynch mob.

Decades later, this Florida city was where Trayvon Martin, a black 17- year-old stepped out of his father's condo into the night on February 26, 2012. Tall for his age (6'3") and skinny, the teenager weighed only 140 pounds and was a junior at a Miami high school.

It started raining and Trayvon pulled his hoodie over his head. He went through the gates and left the Retreat at Twin Lakes, a condominium community where he was visiting his father at the apartment he shared with his fiancé and her son. Water splashed under his sneakers as the teen hurried down the street toward the 7-Eleven.

Once inside the store, Trayvon took an Arizona Iced Tea from the cooler. He placed it on the counter and selected a bag of Skittles from the candy rack. The clerk waited patiently while the youth dug into the pocket of his jeans for the money.

As Trayvon left the store, his cell phone rang. He frowned at the screen. Rachel Jeantel had already called a few times. Still, he decided to talk to her. Ordinarily, he would have tapped the speaker icon, but the rain was pouring down on him; and so, he pressed the cell to his ear to keep it dry.

NOTE: *These excerpts of the conversation between Rachel Jeantel and Trayvon were taken from her testimony while she was Witness #12 for the prosecution.*

Rachel: "What's up?"
Trayvon: "Nothing. Check to see if the game's on."
Rachel: "Okay."

With his head bowed to keep his face dry, Trayvon hurried through the gate back into The Retreat at Twin Lakes. Meanwhile, on a parallel street, a car was patrolling the neighborhood. The driver was George Zimmerman ("GZ"). He was 28 and belonged to a neighborhood watch group, and he was out looking for intruders. Born to a Puerto Rican mother and a white father, GZ was 5'8" and a beefy 200 pounds.

Suddenly, the rain poured down. With his head bowed, Trayvon scurried across the street and into the headlights of GZ's car. The neighborhood watchman hit the brakes and scowled at the stranger. Trayvon stared back at him and the man punched 911 into his cell phone.

The time was 7:11 p.m.

NOTE: This is from the transcript of that call:
GZ: "This guy looks like he's up to no good."
Operator: "Can you describe him?"
GZ: "A black teen wearing a dark hoodie. Shit! He's running!"
Operator: "Are you following him?"
GZ: "Yeah."
Operator: "We don't need you to do that."
GZ: "Okay."

Disgruntled, GZ ended the call and continued to follow the teen anyway.

The time was 7:13 p.m.

Trayvon became aware the car was following him and dashed down a sidewalk and behind a building. GZ jumped out of his car in hot pursuit.

Trayvon resumed talking on his cell, and this was Rachel Jeantel's version of their conversation:

Trayvon: "Some creepy ass cracker is following me."
Rachel: "Maybe he's a molester."

Trayvon: "Don't even talk like that."
Rachel: "Where are you now?"
Trayvon: "Near the mailboxes."

Suddenly, she heard an angry shout.

GZ: "What are you doing around here?"
Trayvon: "Why are you following me, man? Get off! Get off!"

The phone went silent and Rachel was worried.

Rachel: "Trayvon!"

He didn't answer.

It's reasonable to assume that GZ had tried to pat Trayvon down for a weapon. Until the white man had put his hands on him, the black kid would have shown him respect that he would have shown any adult.

According to the 911 calls from eyewitnesses who looked out their windows and ear witnesses who didn't see anything, this is what happened next:

On the sidewalk, man and boy wrestled. They ended up in the wet grass. Several residents heard screams that sounded like "Help!" in a high-pitched voice. Jonathan Good came out of his condo to investigate. In the darkness, he saw the silhouettes of two people tussling on the ground. He said they were wrestling using mixed martial arts (MMA).

"What's going on?" he said.

"Help me subdue this guy," one of the fighters said. Florida was still the Deep South, and so it would not have made any sense for Trayvon to ask a white man to help him subdue another white man.

Good issued a warning "I'm calling the police!" before retreating into his first-floor apartment. Again, applying logic to the time and place—nighttime in the Deep South—if Trayvon were on top beating GZ's brains out, it's hard to imagine that a white male bystander would not have intervened to save him.

The fact that Good went back inside and left the status quo was enough to support the conclusion that the black kid was getting the worst ofit. It is also a big clue as to what had really happened: Both Good and GZ claimed that Trayvon was silent throughout the struggle.

Although Trayvon was a stranger in the area, he knew how badly things could go for him. Therefore, it was more likely that he had tried to let this other white man know that he was the victim. Most likely, he would have had cried out, "Help me, call my father, he lives here!"

However, Good testified that he had turned his back and went back inside to call 911. While he and other residents were on the phone with the operator, there were screams of terror in a high-pitched voice before a shot rang out in the night.

The time was now 7:17 p.m.

Six minutes had passed since GZ had first seen Trayvon and called 911. A single hollow point bullet from the neighborhood watchman's 9 mm semi-automatic handgun had exploded in Trayvon's heart, killing him, if not instantly, within seconds.

Suddenly, Jonathan Manola ventured from his condo. This "good Samaritan" offered to call 911. However, GZ told him he had already called. Truth is, the killer didn't tell the operator that he had shot the boy. Help was not on the way and showing concern for the shooter, Manola took pictures of GZ's bloody nose and the back of his head but did nothing to help the dying child sprawled in the grass.

The first police officer arrived. He found Trayvon face down and motionless. GZ quickly confessed and in the same breath, claimed self-defense. The killer said he had a license to carry a concealed weapon and calmly surrendered his semi-automatic weapon.

Stunned, the police officer spun GZ around and cuffed him. When Manola offered to call GZ's wife, the officer consented. Then the killer gave the good Samaritan this cryptic message to deliver: "Tell her I shot a guy."

That was a curious message coming from a man on his way to jail. The more usual and appropriate things to say would have been, "Tell her I'm okay," or "Something terrible happened," or "Ask her to please meet me at the police station." Instead, "Tell her I shot a guy" sounded less like a message from a concerned husband but more like a veiled threat that carried the implication, "I will shoot you too." After all, GZ's wife Shellie had left him the night before because, as she later explained, she was afraid of him. And studies have shown that leaving your husband was the most dangerous moment in an abusive relationship.

The words "Tell her I shot a guy" may have reverberated all through Shellie's body and filled her with terror.

The arresting officer took GZ to a cruiser and ushered him into the back seat. As more police officers arrived at the scene, they rushed to Trayvon to administer CPR. But it was too late. His heart had stopped beating.

For several hours, GZ was left alone in the patrol car with plenty of time to concoct a story, if he didn't already know what he was going to say. Cool and showing no remorse, GZ was driven to the station. During his video statement, he persuaded the officers that he had acted in self-defense. The next day they took him back to the scene of the shooting, where he repeated his story in a second video statement. Once more, he persuaded them to release him.

Weeks later, during a televised interview with his lawyer, Mark O'Mara sitting beside him, GZ talked about killing Trayvon. The child killer absolved himself from all blame and added the chilling comment, "It was God's will."

2

THE PUBLIC DEMANDS JUSTICE

When GZ arrived at the Sanford police station following his arrest for shooting Trayvon Martin, he knew he was among friends. Florida was one of the seven Deep South states that had seceded from the Union to protest Lincoln's inauguration, and since then, the state had a history of letting whites get away with killing blacks. And so, Trayvon's confessed killer was smug during his interrogation. All the volunteer night watchman believed he had to do was stick to his story that he had shot the teenager in self- defense and he was going home.

Unfortunately for Trayvon's loved ones, GZ was right. His version of what happened was accepted by the police. Except for one. Chris Serino, the lead investigator, suggested that GZ might have committed manslaughter for negligently killing Trayvon. Since Serino's opinion was against the overwhelming sentiment at the station, the neighborhood watchman was allowed to go home.

However, when GZ got there, it was no bed of roses. Callers threatened his life 24-7 prompting the confessed killer and his wife, Shellie Zimmerman, who had returned to him, to flee to a trailer deep in the woods. While the furor raged in the news from outraged blacks and civil rights organizations demanding that charges be filed against him for murder, GZ and Shellie, who was also terrified of her husband, hunkered down and sweated it out.

Meanwhile, Norm Wolfinger, the Florida state attorney for Seminole County, was also under siege. Wolfinger sided with the Sanford police and was adamant that GZ had killed the teenager in self-defense. For a month, the state attorney withstood the public furor against that opinion. Finally, he gave up and withdrew from the case, explaining that he wanted "to tone down the rhetoric."

Surprising the outraged public who were demanding justice, Governor Rick Scott swiftly replaced Wolfinger with Special Prosecutor Angela Corey. She had a reputation for being a badass, and the community sighed in collective relief with Trayvon's parents. Hopes were high that GZ would be held accountable for killing an unarmed boy in cold blood. Corey met with Sybrina Fulton and Tracy Martin, prayed with them, and promised to do everything in her power to see that justice was done.

Trayvon was slain on February 26, 2012, and by April, Corey announced that she had picked her team of Bernie De La Rionda, John Guy, and Richard Mantei from her staff at the state attorney's office.

3

GZ IS CHARGED WITH SECOND-DEGREE MURDER

On April 12, 2012, Special Prosecutor Angela Corey filed an affidavit with the court and announced that GZ was charged with second-degree murder. That was her first and biggest mistake. The confessed killer should have been charged with manslaughter.

It was the usual tactic for the prosecutors to tack on a "lesser included offense" like manslaughter to ensure that the defendant was convicted of something. It made no sense that Corey's team, with 95 years of criminal trials among them, chose to depart from this practice, especially since Florida was a "Stand Your Ground" state where 73% of whites who killed blacks were set free when they pleaded self-defense.

Unfortunately, black women didn't receive the same treatment.

Among others whom Corey had zealously prosecuted, Marissa Alexander was sent to prison for 20 years for simply firing a warning shot over her husband's head during a domestic dispute.

Whereas, manslaughter required the prosecutors to prove three elements that the crime had been committed, second-degree murder required them to prove five. Therefore, when Corey decided against adding manslaughter to the charge of second-degree murder against GZ, as a lesser included offense, she made her team's job of convicting him much harder.

MANSLAUGHTER

To establish that GZ had committed the crime of manslaughter, the prosecutors had to prove the following three elements beyond a reasonable doubt:

1. That Trayvon Martin was killed.
2. That GZ was negligent or accidentally killed Trayvon.
3. That killing Trayvon was not excused or justifiable by law.

SECOND-DEGREE MURDER

To establish that GZ had committed the crime of second-degree murder, the prosecutors had to prove the following five elements beyond a reasonable doubt:

1. That Trayvon Martin was killed.
2. That Trayvon Martin was killed by GZ.
3. That Trayvon Martin was killed by GZ while committing another crime.
4. That killing Trayvon was not excusable or justifiable by law.
5. That when GZ killed Trayvon Martin, he had a depraved mind and showed no regard for human life.

4

MEET THE JUDGE, PROSECUTORS AND THE DEFENSE

THE JUDGE

JUDGE DEBRA NELSON

When GZ was charged with second-degree murder, Judge Kenneth R. Lester, who presided over the arraignment, released him on a $150,000 bail. Days later, the court revoked it after discovering that GZ and his wife had concealed money that they had raised online for his defense. Based on the disparaging remarks Judge Lester made during the hearing about GZ's deception, Lead Defense Counsel Mark O'Mara filed a motion against him for bias and got him removed from the case.

Judge Debra Nelson replaced Lester. She graduated from a Texas law school in 1979 and moved to Florida where she got a job with the state's attorney. Nelson left to go into private practice and then in 1991 she was appointed by Governor Jeb Bush to the circuit court. By the time she presided over GZ's trial, Judge Nelson had served 14 years on the bench.

Presiding over the GZ murder trial propelled her into the national spotlight.

THE PROSECUTORS

SPECIAL PROSECUTOR ANGELA COREY

In 1979, the same year Judge Nelson graduated in Texas, Corey received her law degree from Florida State University. She went into private practice until 1981 when she was hired by the Florida state's attorney. Over the next 26 years, Corey taught courses for the police academy, was active in her Episcopal church, and reportedly tried 50 homicide cases. She enjoyed a reputation for being a "badass" until she was fired by her boss, then State's Attorney Harry Shorstein for planning to run against him in his bid for re- election.

In 2008, Shorstein bowed out of the race and Corey defeated his handpicked successor to become a state attorney for Clay, Duval, and Nassau counties. In March 2012, Governor Rick Scott named Angela Corey as the special prosecutor and sent her to Sanford in Seminole County to investigate whether charges should be filed against GZ for killing Trayvon.

Meanwhile, churches, civil rights groups, and other organizations led by Reverend Al Sharpton and other national figures, held press conferences, circulated petitions, marched in protest and participated in rallies across the country. Finally, on April 12, 2012, Corey announced that she had charged GZ with second-degree murder. From her staff at the state attorney's office in Jacksonville, she selected her team of prosecutors: Bernie De La Rionda, John Guy, and newcomer Richard Mantei.

Corey met with Trayvon's parents, Sybrina Fulton and Tracy Martin, prayed with them and vowed to work tirelessly to get justice for his family. Unfortunately, it was a promise she failed to keep.

Three years after GZ was set free, Florida voters kicked Corey out of office. Melissa Nelson (no relation to Judge Debra Nelson) was elected and replaced Corey as state's attorney for Florida's Fourth Circuit Court.

Corey continues to insist that "how GZ had killed Trayvon Martin fit the bill of second-degree murder and we charged what we believed we could prove." While her statement could have been true, her team mishandled the trial from start to finish and behaved like rank amateurs who had never set foot inside a criminal courtroom.

BERNIE DE LA RIONDA

At four years old, Bernie De La Rionda was a refugee from Cuba living with his grandfather in Miami's Little Havana. When Bernie grew up, he went to law school at Florida State University and his first job was working for the state attorney's office for the Fourth Circuit. That's where he met Angela Corey. Over a span of 25 years, he impressed her with his zeal and work ethic.

Following the not guilty verdict, De La Rionda claimed that out of 96 murder trials, he had only lost two. That was a better record than Corey had but it was contradicted by his lackluster, almost uncaring, performance during GZ's murder trial.

Six years after GZ was acquitted, State's Attorney Melissa Nelson, who had defeated Corey's re-election bid, accepted De La Rionda's early retirement at age 61 and issued this baffling statement: "Bernie's dedication and resolve in the courtroom were matched only by the care and compassion he showed victims outside of it." Meanwhile, De La Rionda, looking worn out and much older than his years, was interviewed puttering around his garage among boxes of his old cases.

JOHN GUY

John Guy failed in his efforts to get into graduate school and become a psychologist. On a whim, he applied to the law school at Florida State University and was accepted. During the summers, he was hired as an intern at the Florida State's Attorney office. In 1993, he graduated, took the bar exam, and began his career with two other Florida State alumni: Angela Corey and Bernie De La Rionda.

After losing the GZ trial, Guy continued in his job as a prosecutor and occasionally applied to the judicial nominating committee. Persistence paid off in 2006 when Governor Rick Scott appointed him to fill an opening in the family law division of the Fourth Circuit Court, where Guy still serves as a judge.

RICHARD W. MANTEI

In 1995, Richard W. Mantei graduated from Michigan University Law School and passed the Florida Bar Exam. In 2013 he became the junior member on Angela Corey's team. Three years after losing the GZ case, he suffered a stroke but recovered quickly. Mantei is presently in private practice and no longer works for Florida state's attorney.

LOOKING BACK FROM 2020:

It appears the dismal failure of the trial of Trayvon Martin's killer took a heavy toll on the prosecutors. Perhaps, they suffered from tremendous guilt. If that's true, the only way to unburden themselves is to admit the truth that they blew the high-profile case and accept the responsibility for setting GZ free to terrorize more people.

COUNSEL FOR THE DEFENSE

MARK O'MARA

In 1982, Lead Defense Counsel Mark O'Mara, the son of a fire chief, graduated from law school at Florida State University. He shares this alma mater with three of the prosecutors: Special Prosecutor Angela Corey, Bernie De La Rionda, and John Guy. O'Mara began his career as a prosecutor in Seminole County. Twenty-one years later, he would sit at the table across from his three college mates and defend GZ for killing Trayvon Martin.

Of all the lawyers on the case, O'Mara held the most credentials. His board certifications include criminal trials and family law. He taught at Harvard Law; at his alma mater, Florida State University; and at other universities and colleges. O'Mara is a certified mediator in civil and family law. He was president of the National Trial Lawyers Association and is a member of seven state bar associations, including Florida, Texas, Georgia, North Carolina, South Carolina, Arkansas, and Alabama.

Following the GZ trial, O'Mara did a short stint as a legal commentator for CNN and specialized in mass torts to hold large corporations accountable for their defective products. Too bad, he didn't hold GZ accountable to pay his legal fees.

DON WEST

Don West graduated in 1980 from the University at Buffalo Law School. He became a public defender and did trials for 25 years. West's skills in Florida's high-profile cases earned him a listing in the professional magazine Super Lawyers. That's when Mark O'Mara, a long-time friend, chose West to second-chair him during the GZ trial. West explained his philosophy, "Lawyers win cases because of hard work and by knowing what they are doing." However, West behaved like he didn't know what he was doing with his lame joke in the defense's opening statement. It's doubtful that he had O'Mara's approval before he stepped in front of the six female jurors and declared, "Knock-knock. Who's there? George Zimmerman. George Zimmerman who? All right, good, you're on the jury."

West's joke landed with a thud. Every time the abrasive West cross-examined a witness, especially Rachel Jeantel, O'Mara winced and appeared suppress the impulse to fire him.

5

THE LAWYER'S OATH

There is a glaring difference between the lawyer's oath that I took to practice law in Ohio and the Florida oath that GZ's prosecutors took. While Ohio requires members of the bar to be competent during their representations of clients, Florida does not. Although the Deep South state's oath is much longer, no obligations to clients are mentioned except the requirements to keep their secrets and not steal their money.

> **NOTE:** *The Ohio lawyer's oath used to require us to represent our clients "zealously." This provision was deleted after some of my colleagues took their zeal too far and practiced a "scorched earth" type of law where they would do anything to win.*

OHIO LAWYER'S OATH

"I hereby (swear or affirm) that I will support the Constitution and the laws of the United States and the Constitution and the laws of Ohio, and I will abide by the Code of Professional Responsibility. In my capacity as an attorney and officer of the Court, I will conduct myself with dignity and civility and show respect toward judges, court staff, clients, fellow professionals, and all other persons. I will honestly, faithfully, and competently discharge the duties of an attorney-at-law. (Adding "So help me God" is optional.)"

FLORIDA LAWYER'S OATH

"I do solemnly swear: I will support the Constitution of the United States and the Constitution of the State of Florida. I will maintain the respect due to courts of justice and judicial officers. I will not counsel or maintain any suit or proceedings which shall appear to me to be unjust, nor any defense except such as I believe to be honestly debatable under the law of the land. I will employ for the purpose of maintaining the causes confided to me such means only as are consistent with truth and honor and will never seek to mislead the judge or jury by any artifice or false statement of fact or law. I will maintain the confidence and preserve inviolate the secrets of my clients and will accept no compensation in connection with their business except from them or with their knowledge and approval. To opposing parties and their counsel, I pledge fairness, integrity, and civility, not only in court, but also in all written and oral communications."

6

SIX WOMEN ON THE JURY

Six women were selected by the prosecution and defense teams and then Judge Nelson concealed their identities from the public. For their protection, she assigned them numbers and letters.

Here are some facts about these jurors that were released after the trial was over:

B29: She was a young woman of Hispanic origin, had eight children, and was a certified nursing assistant. Her family were newcomers from Chicago, where shootings were common. That's why she said she didn't pay much attention to the news about Trayvon being killed.

B37: She was a white woman, aged fifty, with grown children. Her husband was an attorney and she was a store manager. During questioning she joked that she didn't know much about the Trayvon Martin killing because her newspapers ended up at the bottom of her bird's cage without being read. She expressed doubts about the types of guns permitted on the streets and said those with concealed carry permits should get training. Because she had been called to serve on juries several times before, it seemed like she was eager to finally be selected. However, the prosecutors didn't pick up on that. Their lack of concern about her came back on them after the acquittal when she expressed strong opinions to the media supporting the not guilty verdict and blamed Trayvon for his own killing.

B51: This older white woman lived in Seminole County, where Trayvon was killed. She was the only juror with no children, but her relatives lived nearby. She initially said GZ probably did something wrong. However in the final vote she found him not guilty. Perhaps her remarks during jury selection that cast doubt on the killer's innocence and how the investigation was mishandled might have been intended to get her out of jury duty. Unfortunately, the prosecutors let her slip into the box and helped to decide GZ's fate.

B76: This middle-aged white woman was a real estate rental agent who had lived in Florida for a long time. This was another juror with connections to lawyers. One of her children was one and because of this she had a strong influence on the jury. During jury selection (voir dire), she pointed at Sybrina Fulton and asked, "Is that his mom?" Prosecutors moved to strike her for possible bias, however, Judge Nelson denied it. Their arguments for exclusion were lame. They should have presented supporting case law.

E6: This middle-aged white woman said she went to church often and enjoyed gardening. She was married, and after hearing about Trayvon being slain, she warned her two kids about talking to strangers. She was tearful when she admitted that she was a victim of domestic violence. Prosecutors asked to strike her from the jury when she was too familiar with the names of potential witnesses. Again, they failed to back up their arguments with case law and Judge Nelson denied their motion to exclude her.

E40: This was the fifth white woman on the jury, who only recently moved to Seminole County from Iowa, where she had previously come in contact with few minorities. She claimed not to know much about Trayvon

Martin's shooting. However, she mentioned some details that contradicted this. It's possible that she was eager to get on the jury. Once more, the prosecutors dropped the ball and let her slide into a seat in the box.

THE ALTERNATE JURORS

Four alternate jurors also sat through the trial. Two of them were men whose expertise about bullies, punks, and fighting were sorely needed by the prosecutors to enlighten the six women on those issues, especially when the defense counsel mispresented how normal men behaved under those circumstances. Also, the younger male said that GZ should have waited for the police instead of following Trayvon. The prosecutors definitely needed this alternate to balance the bias in favor of GZ that had been expressed by some female jurors.

7

THE BASIC STEPS
OF A MURDER TRIAL

Crime shows like *The Practice, Law and Order,* and *Matlock and Perry Mason*—my favorite from back in the day—depicted, more or less accurately, how the justice system works during a murder case.

1. THE ARREST

The case starts with the arrest of a suspect. Crimes are defined by law and are written down in city ordinances, State and federal codes. When a police officer witnesses a crime or has reason to believe a crime has been committed based on an injured victim or other credible witness, he detains the suspect and reads him his Miranda rights to remain silent and have a lawyer appointed if he can't afford one. If charges are filed, the suspect gets a new name, "the defendant."

On February 26, 2012, GZ was arrested at the scene after he shot 17-year-old Trayvon Martin. When the first police officer arrived at The Retreat at Twin Lakes in Sanford, Florida, the killer confessed and surrendered his 9 mm Kel-Tec semi-automatic pistol.

Following his interview at the police station, the Sanford Police Department decided not to file any charges against GZ for killing Trayvon Martin. In response, the public outcry for justice swept across the nation.

2. BAIL

Bail (aka bond), is a payment to ensure a defendant shows up for all court appearances. The court sets the amount according to the seriousness of the offense. Violent crimes come with the highest bails. Most defendants pay a bondsman a fee of 10 percent to get released until the trial date. However, a defendant can save money by paying the clerk in cash or with a lien on someone's real estate. If the defendant misses a court date, that's a separate crime and the bail is forfeited.

Judges have wide discretion to increase or lower bail, or to release a defendant with no criminal record on his own recognizance without paying anything. Of course, if the crime is murder or another serious felony like arson, the judge can deny bail completely depending on the level of threat the defendant poses to the community.

On April 20, 2012, following two months of controversy in the media, GZ got on the witness stand at his bail hearing. He said he was sorry for the loss of Sybrina Fulton and Tracy Martin's son and the confessed killer was released on a $150,000 bond with an electronic monitoring device attached to his leg.

3. THE ARRAIGNMENT: GUILTY OR NOT GUILTY?

At arraignment before a judge or magistrate, the charges against the defendant are read out loud. To save time, some lawyers waive the reading for their clients. The defendant can plead guilty, not guilty, or no contest.

No contest means the facts are not disputed, but the defendant gets to explain what happened. The judge then typically finds him guilty anyway.

In high-profile cases, a defendant sometimes does not appear at his arraignment. For instance, GZ did not, and Mark O'Mara entered a "not guilty" plea for him.

4. PRESENTENCE REPORT

After a defendant pleads "guilty" or is found guilty pursuant to a no contest plea, the judge will order the probation department to investigate his prior convictions, job history, and living circumstances. This is called a presentence report and helps the court determine the appropriate sentence and fine to make him pay.

However, if a defendant pleads "not guilty" like GZ did, the court will set the first of several pre-trials with the prosecutor to work out a plea. If no deal is made, the case proceeds to trial and the prosecutor has to provide "discovery," which includes all the evidence they collected during their investigation, including all "exculpatory evidence" that proves the defendant is innocent.

At trial, the defendant has the right not to testify and doesn't have to prove anything or produce any evidence. The burden is on the prosecutors to prove that the defendant is guilty of the crime beyond a reasonable doubt.

5. PRELIMINARY HEARING AND THE GRAND JURY

When a suspect is accused of killing somebody, the police conduct an investigation. The prosecutor or state's attorney reviews the findings, and if there is enough proof that the defendant unlawfully took somebody's life, charges are filed in the court.

If the defendant pleads not guilty, he has the right to a preliminary hearing ("PH") for a judge to determine if there is enough evidence to put him on trial. In a municipal court, when the crime is a felony that exceeds its jurisdiction, the court must determine if there is reasonable cause to have the defendant bound over for indictment by the grand jury of a county common pleas court.

During a PH, the burden is on the prosecutor to call witnesses and present evidence to prove the defendant most likely committed the crime. The defendant retains the right to remain silent, and his counsel can cross-examine the prosecution witnesses.

The PH is an opportunity for the defense to find out how weak or strong the prosecution's evidence is. If the judge is not persuaded that the defendant has committed the crime, the defendant will be set free. However, if the judge finds reasonable cause exists, the defendant is held for trial or bound over to the grand jury for an indictment.

The grand jury reviews the evidence and can refuse to indict which is called a "No Bill." It's extremely rare and there is a joke that the grand jury will indict a cheese sandwich if a prosecutor asks them to.

In GZ's case, the special prosecutor bypassed the grand jury and filed a charge of second-degree murder against him. Judge Mark Herr reviewed Corey's supporting affidavit and found probable cause to put Trayvon Martin's confessed killer on trial.

6. BENCH OR JURY TRIAL?

Every defendant accused of a crime with a jail sentence is entitled to a trial by a jury of his peers. A defendant who waives that right is entitled to a "bench trial." That means the judge will hear the evidence and decide the case. Otherwise, a group of citizens are summoned for jury duty. During "*voir dire*," which in French means "to see and to say," the potential jurors are asked questions by the defense and prosecution to select fair and impartial citizens from the pool.

Don't believe it. Both sides try to stack the deck with folks they hope will be sympathetic to their side. After the jury is selected, the judge determines which evidence will be allowed during the trial. Both sides make motions and cross-motions to get their evidence admitted and block the opponent from getting theirs approved.

After the documents and witnesses are selected, each side makes an opening statement to the jury. What the lawyers say is not considered evidence. It's just their version of what happened and what they believe the evidence will show during the trial. Regardless, studies show that most jurors make up their minds about the guilt or innocence of the defendant during the opening statement. Therefore, the lawyers should bring their "A" games. Unfortunately, John Guy cursed at the jury and pranced around like a mad man. From there, it was downhill for the GZ prosecutors.

Following the opening statements, the prosecution goes first and puts on a "prima facie case" to prove the defendant is guilty. To dispute it, the defense cross-examines the prosecution witnesses. Then the prosecution then gets another shot with questions during the "redirect examination." When the prosecution's last witness leaves the stand, the prosecution "rests" its case.

Then it's the defense's turn. Witnesses testify on direct examination and the prosecution gets to cross-examine them. The defense can follow up with questions on redirect before resting its case.

If the defense believes the prosecution has not made its case to convict the defendant beyond a reasonable doubt, it moves for a "directed verdict," which is rarely granted by any judge. Once a jury is impaneled, the court prefers to let them deliberate to reach a verdict.

After both sides have presented their cases, the prosecutors and defense counsel negotiate over the "legal instructions" that the judge will give to the jury that explain the applicable laws. Then each side delivers a "closing argument." The prosecutors will argue that they proved the defendant is guilty beyond a reasonable doubt, and the defense will argue that the defendant is innocent.

Finally, the judge addresses the jury to explain the laws they must apply. The judge will reiterate that it's the jury's duty to determine whom they believe had told the truth and who was lying. The jury will "retire" to deliberate and reach a verdict.

After the first vote, the GZ jurors were evenly hung, 3 to acquit and 3 to convict. But, as everybody knows, they kept deliberating until the "not guilty" votes were unanimous.

7. BEYOND A REASONABLE DOUBT

Criminal and civil trials are similar in how they are conducted. However, the legislators of each state pass their own sets of civil rules of procedure and criminal rules of procedure that differ in many ways. For example, proving someone has committed a crime requires a higher standard of proof which is "beyond a reasonable doubt" than in a civil case for damages to your property where the standard of proof is by "a preponderance of the evidence". That means that if more than half of the evidence shows you owe damages than shows that you don't, you lose.

It should be tougher to prove you committed a criminal act because putting a defendant in jail and depriving them of their freedom is irreversible. You can never get back the time lost while locked up in jail but you can always get more money.

"Beyond a reasonable doubt" is not beyond all doubt, just the doubts a reasonable man would still have after hearing all the evidence and applying their common sense. The "reasonable man" standard is a holdover from when only men were allowed to be on juries.

8. SENTENCING

If the defendant is found not guilty by the jury, he's free to go home. Otherwise, the judge decides on the sentence to be served. So, how does a judge decide? Following the guilty verdict, the court will order a pre-sentence report from the probation department. It will include the details of the crime, including the weapons used and the defendant's prior convictions, if any. The prosecutors will recommend a sentence, and a repeat offender who committed a violent crime will typically get a harsher sentence than a first-time, nonviolent defendant.

"Mitigating circumstances" where the defendant was under stress and nobody was hurt sometimes result in a lighter sentence. However, by law, "mandatory sentencing" in "aggravating circumstances" where there was violence or use of a deadly weapon can increase prison time.

9. THE RIGHT TO APPEAL

Every defendant convicted of murder has an automatic to appeal to a higher court to reverse it. However, because GZ was found not guilty, no appeal was necessary. And that's why appellate procedures are not covered in this book.

8

MISTAKES BEFORE THE TRIAL STARTED

Before a prosecutor steps in front of a jury, a lot of work is done for what is called pretrial preparation. It requires tracking down and interviewing witnesses, consultations with the police, and investigating the suspect, his friends, and his family. After this information is gathered and scrupulously reviewed, the prosecutor decides what crime has been committed and files charges against the defendant that can be proved beyond a reasonable doubt.

PRE-TRIAL MISTAKE #1:
The prosecutors did not charge GZ with manslaughter

Special Prosecutor Angela Corey made a terrible mistake in judgment when she charged GZ with second-degree murder. It was much harder to prove than manslaughter, which is a "lesser-included offense" in the crime of second-degree murder. That means the prosecutors had to prove he was guilty of manslaughter, anyway, on the way to proving he was guilty of second-degree murder. When the prosecutors asked the court to add manslaughter, the judge denied the motion for being made out of the required time limit. If Corey had reviewed the local rules for the Eighteenth Circuit Court before she prepared the affidavit, she would have known that no charge could be added later.

Nevertheless, making an unexplained reversal of her ruling, Judge Nelson gave instructions to the jury that included manslaughter.

Unfortunately for the prosecutors and Trayvon's parents, justice was denied when the jury sent a note to the judge during their deliberations asking her to clarify the elements of the lesser included offense. Again, for reasons known only by her, Judge Nelson refused and left the jury to their own interpretations. Possibly irked that the judge had failed to respond to them, the six women on the jury found GZ not guilty.

Although Judge Nelson gave the prosecutors a break by allowing manslaughter to be included in her instructions to the jury, the prosecutors were not prepared to take advantage of it. They didn't adequately explain the elements of the crime to the jury either during their opening statement or closing arguments.

This blunder was the most fatal blunder to the prosecution.

PRE-TRIAL MISTAKE #2:

The prosecutors waived "stand your ground"

To this day, most people blame Florida's "Stand Your Ground" law for getting GZ off the hook for killing Trayvon Martin. But it's not true. During pretrial negotiations, the defense waived the application of Florida "Stand Your Ground" law. Many people will be surprised to find that the defense never used it during the trial.

Lead Defense Counsel O'Mara understood what the prosecutors did not. Namely, that the "Stand Your Ground" law would apply to both the killer and his victim. If George Zimmerman had the right to stand his ground, so did Trayvon Martin.

This was worrisome to O'Mara because Trayvon's right to stand his ground and beat up GZ was an equalizer, and that was a major stumbling block to get an acquittal based on GZ's claim of self-defense.

Because the prosecutors never took the time to understand how "Stand Your Ground" actually worked, they were stuck with the public outcry against it and the fear that it would be used to set GZ free. And so, these so- called seasoned litigators fell into O'Mara's trap. They waived the application of "Stand Your Ground" during the trial and lost an opportunity to destroy GZ's claim of self-defense.

The defense team could hardly contain themselves. Since "Stand Your Ground" would have cut both ways, the prosecutors could have argued successfully that Trayvon Martin had the exact same right not to retreat as his killer.

Without this explanation by the prosecution, O'Mara assumed the jury would apply "Stand Your Ground" in GZ's favor anyway. According to remarks made after the not guilty verdict, the lead defense counsel was right. Several of the jurors believed that GZ did not have an obligation to retreat, and therefore he had the right to shoot and kill Trayvon. The prosecutors had failed to explain and the six women in the box didn't consider that Trayvon also had the right to stand his ground and to use deadly force like bashing GZ's head on the sidewalk.

PRE-TRIAL MISTAKE #3:
The prosecutors did not charge GZ with conspiracy to commit perjury

GZ and his wife, Shellie Zimmerman, raised $130,000 on the internet for his defense. To get a lower bail for him, Shellie lied to the court under oath that they were broke. However, the telephones at the jail were bugged.

While GZ and his wife thought they were slick and talked in code, referring to their PayPal account as "Peter Pan," an investigation was done and the money was discovered.

Convicting GZ for suborning perjury and both Zimmermans for conspiracy to commit perjury and a fraud on the court was a sure thing. For unknown reasons, the prosecutors rejected this opportunity to nail GZ. Instead, they charged Shellie Zimmerman with perjury, but no additional charges were filed against GZ. Why not?

Every prosecutor's goal is to impeach the defendant and expose him as a liar to the jury. Why did Corey's team pass up a chance to destroy GZ's credibility when it was handed to them on a platter? If they had filed charges of suborning perjury and conspiracy to commit perjury, the defense counsel would have been eager to fold their tent and sit down at the table to plead GZ out to manslaughter.

Instead, the prosecutors let GZ slide on a sure conviction. Why?

Whose side were they on?

PRE-TRIAL MISTAKE #4:

The prosecutors delayed prosecuting GZ's wife until his trial was over

The prosecutors missed the opportunity to use the threat of charging GZ's wife with perjury, conspiracy to commit perjury, and a fraud on the court to get her to roll over on him. There was a history of domestic disputes between the couple, and it was common knowledge that Shellie Zimmerman was miserable in her marriage. However, she was terrified of GZ, and if Corey's team had assured her that her husband was going to do a long stretch of hard time, she probably would have cooperated with the prosecutors to help convict him.

It's baffling that these prosecutors didn't even try to convince her to take their side. Although by law a wife can't be compelled to testify against her husband, she is allowed to do so voluntarily. Especially if it's going to keep her out of prison. If she had refused to cooperate, the prosecutors could have immediately charged Shellie and convicted her so that they could use her as a witness in GZ's trial. Not to testify about privileged information—what her husband told her about killing Trayvon—but to destroy GZ's credibility by telling the jury about their conspiracy to commit perjury and fraud.

What was Angela Corey's team thinking?

PRE-TRIAL MISTAKE #5:

The prosecutors did not dig into GZ's abusive past with other women

GZ's marriage was in turmoil. Shellie Zimmerman had left him the night before he killed Trayvon and fled to her father's house. Her family could have provided the prosecutors with negative information about their son-in- law if they had asked! GZ's father-in-law didn't think much of him and may have provided them with leads to GZ's prior romances for them to contact.

Abusers don't become abusive overnight. It's possible that GZ had a string of terrorized women in his past who might have been willing to come forward and testify about his violent tendencies. Also, had the prosecutors tailed his wife for a few days, they might have discovered a lot more. She might have had a lover or confided to friends or a hair stylist information about Trayvon's killing. Repeating what she had told them would have been a waiver of a wife's privilege not to testify against her husband.

PRE-TRIAL MISTAKE #6:

The prosecutors did not investigate GZ's vigilante friends and associates

GZ claimed to be a volunteer watchman because he wanted to protect his neighbors at The Retreat at Twin Lakes. The prosecutors accepted his story and failed to examine his associations with vigilantes to find out what was really going on inside the killer's head. Was he inspired by Charles Bronson's character in the movie *Death Wish*? If he didn't plan to shoot and kill Trayvon, why did GZ carry a gun with deadly hollow point bullets and have an extra bullet in the chamber?

What were his opinions about "Stand Your Ground"? How did he really feel about the police? His remark to 911, "Fucking assholes! They always get away!" showed his frustration with law enforcement. Or was that just part of a clever scheme to cover up his true intention to take the life of a kid he said he had never met before?

It was more likely that GZ had seen Trayvon during previous sweeps of the neighborhood and knew the black kid wasn't a resident. What's more, wearing a hoodie and baggy clothes made him the perfect target. After all, Sanford, Florida was in the Deep South, where whites historically got away with murder.

PRE-TRIAL MISTAKE #7:

They failed to find out who Trayvon Martin really was to inspire them to convict his killer

In an episode of *Law & Order*, the chief prosecutor said that the first question a witness must answer in a murder trial is "Did the victim deserve to die?" If the answer is no, as was the case in the shooting of 17-year-old Trayvon Martin, the prosecutor must bring the victim back to life in the courtroom for the jury to get to know who he was and like him.

In order to tell Trayvon's story, the prosecutors had to get to know Trayvon's family. While Angela Corey met and prayed with his parents, it was just for show. No real connection was made with them, and the special prosecutor didn't seek out Trayvon's friends or make an effort to visit Trayvon's school or the neighborhood where he grew up.

The GZ prosecutors did not do any of those things for Trayvon because they gave up on him from the start. Stereotypes may have prevented them from delving deeper to find out who this youth really was in order to motivate them to convict his killer.

The prosecutors wrongly assumed he was a bad kid. It turned out that Trayvon was an ordinary kid struggling to find himself. Sometimes he experimented with marijuana, scrawled graffiti on walls, and skipped school. But that behavior is hardly uncommon for teenagers of any generation.

Most certainly, that rainy night in Sanford, when GZ began stalking him, Trayvon was in his own world, and distracted while talking on his cell phone with Rachel Jeantel.

Angela Corey's team didn't even bother to bring a life-sized photo of Trayvon to remind the jury what the case was about. They didn't tell Trayvon's story in photos or videos to let the jury get to know who he really was. And the mindless chronological order of their witnesses showed a lack of focus on his loss. Instead of calling Trayvon's mother to testify first or even second, the prosecutors called her as witness #36 of 38 witnesses. She was third from last, as if what she had been through was an afterthought.

Regardless of the judge's instructions not to be swayed by sympathy, it was naïve for the prosecutors to ignore the fact that every juror wants to hear the victim's story. Still, Corey's team passed up the opportunity to show that Trayvon Martin was a real human being with friends and family who loved him despite his faults. His plans, his hobbies, his habits, and the fun things he did were crucial for jurors to understand the loss his family suffered. Also, the Prosecutors failed in their duty to show how much Sybrina's child was going be missed and how much he was going to miss because his life was snuffed out way too soon.

PRE-TRIAL MISTAKE #8:

The prosecutors failed to find GZ's real motive for killing Trayvon

Crime-show watchers know that who did it and why are essential to solving every crime. The GZ prosecutors obviously hadn't watched much television, and so, they failed to understand that not explaining GZ's true motive to the jury was a big hole in their case. Although the resources of the Florida State Attorney's office were at their disposal and universities and civil rights organizations around the world were willing to lend a hand to see that justice was done, Corey's team never reached out for help. Instead of concentrating their efforts on finding out what drove GZ to kill an unarmed teenager, Bernie De La Rionda, John Guy, and Richard Mantie stumbled around like the Three Blind Mice, making mistake after mistake, when they were supposed to be fighting for justice for Trayvon and his family.

Only Angela Corey's team of prosecutors know the reason for their poor performance and they have never admitted publicly why they blew GZ's trial.

PRE-TRIAL MISTAKE #9:

The prosecutors did not know how to put a winning case together

When this author was assigned a case, I sat down and reviewed the file to familiarize myself with the facts and evidence. Next, I would research the law for updates and write down the elements of the crime charged against the defendant that I had to prove. After that, I would review the file a second time and make detailed notes to refer to during interviews with the witnesses and the arresting officer.

I won my first jury trial despite making a few mistakes. For instance, I put the victim on the witness stand and forgot to ask how much the radio console that the defendant had stolen was worth. The value was an element of the crime because $500 or more made the crime a felony. It was a good thing that breaking into a car, which I had already proven through an eyewitness, was also a felony. Otherwise, due to my oversight, the defendant would have gotten off with a much lighter sentence for a misdemeanor.

Although there is no such thing as a perfect trial and minor mistakes can't be avoided, a well-prepared and organized prosecutor can walk into the courtroom with confidence and sail through to a conviction on any case.

To minimize errors, I learned how to organize my cases using a system of colored folders. Blue held a summary of what each of my witnesses would say. Yellow contained my opening statement and closing arguments. Green was for the current status of the law, including the elements of the crime that I had to prove. In my red folder was information about the defendant and the weaknesses in the defense's case. It was also where I kept my questions for cross-examination.

My white folder contained the lynch pin to my success: my trial progress list, the outline of my presentation, the names of my witnesses, and the numbers of the corresponding exhibits that supported their testimony.

After questioning each witness, I checked off their name with a red marker.

If there was another prosecutor on the case with me, who was known as the "second chair," I would give them a duplicate of my white folder.

That way they could mark their copy of my trial progress list to help keep me on track.

My second chair did not need a copy of my other folders because we would have spent many hours critiquing and polishing the entire case backwards and forwards. Then I would place all my folders into a thick manila envelope and carry them to the court. Then I would I present my trial exhibits to the reporter to number and record. The prosecution's evidence starts with the letter "A," while the defense evidence is assigned numbers.

9

MISTAKES THEY MADE
DURING THE TRIAL

PART ONE:
34 UNNECESSARY PROSECUTION WITNESSES

During this author's three decades as a lawyer, most of them as a prosecutor, I have seen few losses where my colleagues let victory slip away due to sloppy work. Most of us rise to the task and perform our duties with diligence. By contrast, Corey's team continually displayed an appalling lack of professionalism while losing the trial of Trayvon Martin's killer.

Furthermore, rather than limit their presentation to the four crucial witnesses who could have proven GZ guilty of killing Trayvon in coldblooded second degree murder, Corey's so-called seasoned prosecutors trotted out 34 unnecessary witnesses who had little relevant information to convey, prolonged the trial, and made it impossible for the six women in the box to sort out the truth to render the correct verdict of guilty beyond a reasonable doubt.

After they lost, the prosecutors tried to absolve themselves of responsibility by saying they had to take the witnesses as they found them. Nonsense! There were 38 witnesses to choose from, and Corey's team had the responsibility to select the witnesses who would best serve their case and forget the rest.

Instead, they summoned 34 witnesses to the stand, most of whom destroyed their case. These lawyers were arrogant, lazy, or just didn't care to put forth the effort to weed out the bad witnesses in order to convict GZ.

The following unnecessary witnesses are listed in the order in which they testified for the prosecution.

Gaps in the sequence of numbers are due to the omission of the names of the four witnesses who were crucial to prove the prosecutors' case. See Chapter 12, How They Could Have Won for analysis of the testimonies of Trayvon's mother Sybrina Fulton, firearms expert Amy Siewert, the arresting officer Timothy Smith, and the medical examiner Shipping Bao.

UNNECESSARY PROSECUTION WITNESS #1:
CHAD JOSEPH

(Trayvon's never- to-be stepbrother)

On June 24, 2013, 15-year-old Chad Joseph was the first witness for the prosecution. It had been over a year since Trayvon Martin was slain. The jury and the rest of the world were on the edge of their seats bursting with pent-up expectations to finally hear the victim's story.

Trayvon's parents were divorced, and his father, Tracy Martin, had a fiancé, who was Chad Joseph's mother. Trayvon was visiting them at The Retreat at Twin Lakes in Sanford, Florida, where GZ was a neighbor. As Chad took the stand, the jurors and the television audience, including me, leaned forward in anticipation. He was the last family member to see Trayvon alive and we were all primed to hear about his family's pain and suffering.

Instead, Chad swiveled in his chair and glanced around as if he were bored. Trayvon's never-to-be stepbrother failed to get sympathy from the jury with his monotone single syllable answers and started the prosecution's side of the story with a whimper instead of a bang.

Unlike competent and zealous prosecutors who spent many hours with their prime witnesses reviewing their testimony to make sure they know what they are going to say and how to say it, Angela Corey's team— Bernie De La Rionda, John Guy, and Richard Mantei—appeared not to care enough to meet with Chad to properly prepare him to testify while the world was watching.

They didn't even tell him to sit up straight in the courtroom, Also, Chad should have been told to avoid certain terminology. For example, he referred to Tracy Martin as his mother's "boyfriend." "Fiancé," "life partner," or "special friend" were more appropriate to describe the romantic relationship between adults. "Boyfriend" sounded undignified.

Unfortunately, the jurors were given the impression that Martin was immature instead of thoughtful and serious-minded. Otherwise, a grown man would not have allowed his fiance's son to refer to him as her "boyfriend."

Even worse, the jury of mostly mothers, was left without an explanation for why a whole night had passed before the family notified the authorities that Trayon hadn't returned to where his father was staying. The prosecutors allowed them to assume that nobody even cared that the 17- year-old was missing.

UNNECESSARY PROSECUTION WITNESS #2:
ANDREW GAUGH
(7-Eleven Clerk)

Although it was interesting to find out where Trayvon had bought the bag of Skittles found in his pocket, the prosecutors followed Chad Joseph's tedious testimony with another ho-hum witness. Andrew Gaugh, the 7-Eleven clerk who sold the candy to Trayvon, was a gum-chewing, lip-smacking mess.

At least Chad Joseph's testimony had a bit of relevance: It proved that Trayvon had just left home to go to the store and before he was shot, he wasn't out prowling the neighborhood as GZ claimed.

UNNECESSARY PROSECUTION WITNESS #3:
SEAN NOFFKE
(911 dispatcher)

Sean Noffke testified that he was the 911 dispatcher who had answered GZ's non-emergency call to report Trayvon in his neighborhood the fatal night of February 26, 2012. Although Noffke's testimony had some relevance to show GZ's state of mind and frustration with the police, this witness wasn't necessary to prove the prosecutor's prima facie case of second-degree murder. As explained previously, four other witnesses could have easily done that and forced the confessed killer to testify to prove his case of self-defense.

Mark O'Mara would have pleaded him out to manslaughter—the lead defense counsel was too shrewd to let his client be destroyed on cross-examination and get convicted of second-degree murder.

Too bad the prosecutors weren't as smart as Mark O'Mara. They failed to devise a strategy to make Trayvon's killer testify.

UNNECESSARY PROSECUTION WITNESS #4: RAMONA RUMPH
(911 Supervisor)

Ramona Rumph was the communications director for the Seminole County Sheriff's Office and was in charge of 911 calls. On June 26, 2013, she testified that GZ made five calls prior to the infamous February 26, 2012 call where he reported seeing a black kid in a hoodie who was "up to no good."

Rumph testified that the other non-emergency calls GZ had made were to alert police about other suspicious youth that the volunteer neighborhood watchman had spotted in his neighborhood.

Prosecutor Richard Mantie wasted precious time calling this witness just so that they could get GZ's prior 911 calls into evidence. They didn't need this witness to do that. Instead, they should have compelled GZ to testify, and if he had lied, this witness could have been called in rebuttal.

Inexplicably, the prosecutors failed to ask Rumph about the second 911 call that GZ made that night after the killing. He deceived his neighbor, Jonathan Manola, when he told him that he had already called 911 to report the shooting. Manola was misled into believing that GZ had summoned help for Trayvon, who lay dying in the grass. Instead, GZ had made a sham call repeating his earlier report of a suspicious character lurking about.

Rumph could have told the jury that GZ didn't mention Trayvon's mortal wounds and exposed GZ's deception. It was a crucial oversight and blunder by the prosecutors. Not only had GZ kept the good Samaritan from calling 911 himself to summon help, the shooter's lack of concern that Trayvon's life was seeping away showed a depraved heart and a reckless disregard for human life. These were two of the elements of second-degree murder that the prosecutors had the burden to prove.

This huge blunder showed that the prosecutors didn't understand what it took to prove a depraved heart and a reckless disregard for human life. No caring person would have chased down a boy with a 9 mm pistol, shot him through the heart, re-holstered his weapon, and coolly participated in a photo shoot while the life drained from his victim.

UNNECESSARY PROSECUTION WITNESS #5:
WENDY DORIVAL
(Sanford Police neighborhood crime watch volunteer coordinator)

Perhaps the prosecutors were too busy to make a streamlined list of necessary witnesses. Among the names they seemed to have picked from a hat was Wendy Dorival, who was the coordinator of Sanford Police Department's neighborhood crime watch volunteers. This unnecessary witness hurt the prosecution's case when she told the jury that GZ had good intentions and was eager to serve his community.

Never help the defense!

UNNECESSARY PROSECUTION WITNESS #6:
DONALD O'BRIEN
(President, Retreat at Twin Lake's Homeowners' Association)

Just like the first four witnesses, Don O'Brien, the president of the homeowners' association at The Retreat at Twin Lakes, was not needed to prove the prosecution's case. On the second day of GZ's trial, O'Brien testified that it was his understanding that neighborhood watch volunteers never followed suspects.

Who cared what he understood? Just the facts, ma'am. That's all that counted.

UNNECESSARY PROSECUTION WITNESS #7:
SERGEANT ANTHONY RAIMONDO
(Sanford police officer)

Sergeant Anthony Raimondo from the Sanford Police SWAT team testified that he was the second officer to arrive on the scene of the shooting at The Retreat at Twin Lakes. It was commendable that he tried to revive Martin by performing CPR. However, John Guy wasted a lot of time asking questions to impress the jury with Raimondo's considerable credentials in law enforcement. The jury was anxious to hear from the first officer on the scene, Timothy Smith, who had arrested GZ following his confession.

However, acting like rookies at their first trial, these prosecutors delayed calling this crucial witness to tell the jury who had killed Trayvon Martin.

UNNECESSARY PROSECUTION WITNESS #8:
DIANA SMITH
(Sanford Police Department crime scene technician)

The prosecutors continued their ineffective and nonsensical presentation of their case by calling Diana Smith, a crime scene technician from the Sanford Police Department. She explained that the evidence collected at the scene proved that Trayvon Martin was killed by GZ. No shit, Sherlock. He had already confessed.

UNNECESSARY PROSECUTION WITNESS #9:
SELENE BAHADOOR
(GZ's neighbor)

Continuing with their parade of useless witnesses to the stand, the prosecution called Selene Bahadoor, who was an "earwitness." She was in her kitchen at The Retreat at Twin Lakes when she heard a noise during the struggle between Trayvon and GZ. She said that the noise sounded like a movement from "left to right"—whatever that meant. She looked out the window and saw two people flailing their arms. She heard a gunshot and saw a body face down in the grass.

The first police officer on the scene, Officer Timothy Smith—who should have been called as the first witness—would have testified about finding Trayvon face down in the grass. Instead, the prosecutors called Bahadoor ahead of him, and the defense chipped away at her credibility, accusing her of bias for liking a Change.org petition on Facebook about getting justice for Trayvon.

UNNECESSARY PROSECUTION WITNESS #10:
JEANNE MANALO
(GZ's neighbor and the wife of Jonathan Manalo, the good Samaritan)

Jeanne Manalo testified on day five of GZ's trial. She lived at The Retreat at Twin Lakes with her husband, Jonathan Manola, and their daughter. She was watching television during the struggle outside her window. When they heard the commotion, her husband told her to mind her own business. And yet, when they heard the gunshot, he went outside by himself. Jeanne looked out the window and saw GZ's face in profile.

Jonathan Manalo went out of his condo, where he dallied with GZ for several minutes and took pictures of his bloody nose and the scrapes on his scalp. Why would a sane man, which Manalo appeared to be when he later testified on direct examination, leave the safety of his home to go to the aid of a stranger who had just shot somebody in his backyard? Neither the police nor the prosecutors ever questioned Jeanne Manalo about this abnormal behavior.

Also, while the prosecutors concentrated on GZ's injuries for being minor, they failed to ask Mrs. Manalo what her husband had told her about how GZ got hurt. Inexplicably, Corey's team never delved into the possibility that there was a conspiracy or cover-up. Because the prosecutors never asked his wife to explain why Jonathan had left the safety of their home to confront a man with a gun or even whether Jonathan knew GZ before that night, the answers remain a mystery.

UNNECESSARY PROSECUTION WITNESS #11:
JAYNE SYRDYKA
(GZ's neighbor)

Continuing their march of witnesses in a mindless chronological order, the prosecutors called Jayne Syrdyka, who lived at The Retreat at Twin Lakes. Before the shooting, she heard two voices, but it was raining and too dark for her to see who was talking from her window. She became upset on the stand listening to her voice on the 911 call she had made. Syrdyka started rambling and contradicted her earlier statements. It was another misstep by the prosecution, and the defense scored a lot of points on cross- examination, destroying what little credibility Syrdyka had left.

UNNECESSARY PROSECUTION WITNESS #12:
RACHEL JEANTEL
(Trayvon's friend)

Except for his killer, teenager Rachel Jeantel testified that she was the last person to talk to Trayvon. She claimed to be on the phone with Martin when he was approached by a white man. (See Chapter 1: "Killing Trayvon Martin.") She was on the stand for eight hours and grilled for the defense by Don West. Jeantel described how Trayvon ran away from a "creepy ass cracker" who was stalking him. Poorly prepared—if at all—by the prosecutors for the intense cross-examination, Jeantel was goaded by West, who made mincemeat of her story. She lost her temper and threatened not to come back for the afternoon session. Of course, she did return for more grilling.

The prosecutors should have enlisted an expert in African American English to assist with Rachel's trial preparation to help them and the jury understand what she was saying. A prime example of this is when Jeantel said she heard Trayvon yell, "Get off! Get off!" Unschooled in black slang, the prosecutors mistakenly interpreted it to prove that GZ was on top of the teenager. However, "Get off!" meant "Move back, you're in my space" or "Take your hands off me!"

GZ had reportedly said, "What are you doing around here?" and then he may have shoved Trayvon to move him along or tried to pat him down for a weapon. It's reasonable to assume that's when Trayvon would have uttered "Get off!"

UNNECESSARY PROSECUTION WITNESS #13:
RAYMOND MACDONALD
(T-Mobile manager)

On day four, the prosecution called Raymond MacDonald to testify about Trayvon's cell phone records and how calls were archived. The jury's eyelids slid down to half-mast. What were these so-called litigators thinking? Twelve previous witnesses had already bored the six women in the box, and still they hadn't heard from Trayvon Martin's mother about her tremendous loss or from the medical examiner about how Trayvon was killed.

UNNECESSARY PROSECUTION WITNESS #14:
JENNA LAUER
(GZ's neighbor)

Jenna Lauer testified on June 27, 2013, the fourth day of the trial. During her call to 911, screams were heard in the background, and when the prosecutors put the tape into evidence, it became known as the "Lauer 911 tape" and provoked a battle between Trayvon's parents and GZ's family about who was screaming. The defense argued that if the jury believed that GZ was screaming, there was reasonable doubt that GZ had maliciously killed Trayvon, which was required to convict him of second-degree murder. The jury believed the identifications by GZ's witnesses more than they believed Trayvon's parents, especially since Tracy Martin first denied that it was his son screaming on the tape, and they found GZ not guilty of the crime.

UNNECESSARY PROSECUTION WITNESS #15:
SELMA MORA
(GZ's neighbor)

Selma Mora was the fourth resident from the The Retreat at Twin Lakes and was a so-called eyewitness to the altercation between Trayvon and GZ. She asked for an interpreter and testified in Spanish that she heard a noise, walked outside, and saw one man on top of another. However, she claimed that she couldn't tell who was who.

During cross-examination, Defense Attorney Mark O'Mara required Mora to get off the stand to reenact how she went outside. Since there wasn't a person in the courtroom who didn't know how people walk, the only purpose that appeared to serve was to allow O'Mara to ogle her large breasts.

UNNECESSARY PROSECUTION WITNESS #16:
GREG MCKINNEY
(camera technician)

Greg McKinney, who testified on the fifth day of GZ's trial, belongs at the top of the prosecution's list of most useless witnesses. He worked for the company that maintained the surveillance cameras at The Retreat at Twin Lakes. It's too bad that the two cameras, including the one by the gate where the majority of the action took place, were not working at the time of the shooting and that the time imprints on the other cameras were off by 18 minutes.

UNNECESSARY PROSECUTION WITNESS #17:
JONATHAN GOOD
(GZ's neighbor)

There was nothing good for the prosecutors in the testimony of John Good, another so-called eyewitness, who claimed that he was watching television when he stepped out of his condominium to investigate a noise. When a voice said, "Help me subdue this guy," Good responded that he was going to call the police. When Good turned to go, he claimed the guy wearing a dark hoodie (Trayvon) was on top of the guy in the red top

(GZ). However, Good's account didn't make sense. Why would the person on the bottom ask for help "to subdue this guy" instead of asking to get him off? Furthermore, considering this struggle was between a black kid and GZ who appeared in the dark to be a white man instead of mixed race, Good's account defied local sensibilities. After all, Florida was part of the Deep South, and there was no way a white man would have walked away and not gone to the aid of a fellow white man who was getting beaten by a black person. By the same token, there was no way that a black kid would have kept beating up a white man in front of another white man who could identify him. Especially since the white man had threatened to call the police. If Trayvon had been on top of GZ, he would have jumped up and ran home to stay out of jail. Trayvon was no country bumpkin. He was born and raised in Miami and he knew how things worked in Florida for blacks. That's why he ran away when GZ first started following him. The teenager was trying to avoid trouble when GZ tracked him down and cornered him.

Inexplicably, these prosecutors never pursued this rational view of what really happened. Also, they never asked Good why he had turned his back on the status quo and gone back inside even though it defied logic that he would have left a white man fighting for his life.

It was a colossal mistake for the prosecutors to put Good on the stand to tell the jury that Trayvon was on top because this allowed them to draw the conclusion that he was the aggressor.

UNNECESSARY PROSECUTION WITNESS #18:
JONATHAN MANALO
(the good Samaritan who took GZ's photos immediately after he shot Trayvon)

On June 28, 2013, the fifth day of the trial, the prosecutors called Jonathan Manalo to the stand. There was never any good reason to allow the jury to hear anything this self-appointed good Samaritan had to say. He hurt their case by portraying GZ as a harmless victim that night in Sanford. His wife, Jeanne, Prosecution Witness #11, had already testified that they were watching television when they heard a gunshot outside. Jonathan told her to mind her own business and stay put in their condo. Suddenly, with no explanation (so she claimed), her husband dashed outside.

On direct examination, Jonathan was not even asked by the prosecutors why he had the sudden urge to rush from the safety of his home to offer his assistance and take pictures of a stranger who had just shot someone. If he wanted money, photos of Trayvon would have fetched a lot more than images of GZ's alleged injuries.

What was Jonathan's real motive for helping a killer who was supposedly a stranger to him? Did Manola hate blacks enough to participate in the crime, either before or after the shooting? Did he punch GZ in the nose to cover up the fact that he was not hurt by Trayvon? Was Manola in fact a friend or an admirer of the neighborhood watchman?

Unless Manola knew GZ and wasn't concerned for his own safety, it made no sense for him to come to his aid. If the good Samaritan shared the killer's values about guns and shooting people, that would explain why he was unaffected by the mortally wounded child lying in the grass.

Once again dropping the ball, these prosecutors failed to ask any questions to find out what prior contacts Manola had with GZ or if they had any gun clubs or organizations in common.

While Angela Corey and her team of prosecutors claimed that they did their best to get GZ convicted, they were not even curious enough to delve into the good Samaritan's background or motives for helping GZ. These prosecutors were so inept that they didn't recognize that Manola held the key to GZ's motive for the killing. When the officer handcuffed the confessed killer, the good Samaritan offered to call his wife, Shellie, for him. GZ told him, "Tell her I shot a guy!"

From a man on his way to jail, that was a very unusual message to send his spouse. "Tell her I'm okay, but something bad happened" or "There was an accident, please meet me at the police station" would have been more appropriate. But "Tell her I shot a guy!" sounded like a veiled threat that implied "I will shoot you, too, if you don't come back to me!" Maybe he had told his wife that he was going to kill her and was now letting her know that he could make good on his threat.

Studies have shown that the most dangerous time in an abusive relationship is when a woman tries to end it. Shellie Zimmerman had left GZ the night before he killed Trayvon. Too bad the prosecutors didn't connect the dots between her leaving and the veiled threat in GZ's message, but apparently his wife got it. Shellie hurried back home to him.

Playing the dutiful wife, she stuck by her husband's side throughout the trial. And then as soon as it was over, she fled again and divorced him, perhaps hoping that the spotlight on GZ would deter him from killing her. She took the gamble and was right. Although he came to her father's home and terrorized them, Trayvon's killer knew the odds were low that he could get away with murder twice. At least so soon.

UNNECESSARY PROSECUTION WITNESS #19:
RICARDO AYALA
(Sanford police officer)

The prosecutors continued their montage of unnecessary witnesses with Officer Ricardo Ayala, who took the stand on June 28, 2013. Ayala was a police officer from the Sanford Police Department who had helped perform CPR on Trayvon. Although his efforts were commendable and Trayvon's parents are very grateful, Officer Ayala's testimony wasn't needed by the prosecutors to establish that GZ had shot and killed their son. He had already confessed to that.

UNNECESSARY PROSECUTION WITNESS #20:
STACEY LIVINGSTON
(Sanford Fire Department)

Stacey Livingston worked for the Sanford Fire Department and was on the scene when Trayvon Martin was pronounced dead. Unfortunately, this was a job for the medical examiner who should have testified instead of Livingston. In a backward move, the prosecutors called their witnesses in the reverse order of importance. The medical examiner, Scott Baio, was called last after seven more witnesses testified. This was an irrational strategy, and the defense team knew victory was in sight.

PROSECUTION WITNESS #21:
TIMOTHY SMITH
(GZ's arresting officer was a crucial witness)

Officer Smith was one of the four witnesses the prosecution needed to prove their case. See Chapter 11, How They Could Have Won.

UNNECESSARY PROSECUTION WITNESS #22:
LINDZEE FOLGATE
(Physician's Assistant)

In yet another move that defied logic, the prosecutors called Lindzee Folgate to testify on June 28, 2013. She was the physician's assistant who examined GZ the day after he killed Trayvon. The prosecutors lacked the good sense to ask her whether GZ's injuries could have been faked.

If she couldn't say that GZ's injuries were self-inflicted, Folgate was useless and shouldn't have been put on the stand.

UNNECESSARY PROSECUTION WITNESS #23:
HIROTAKA NAKASONE
(FBI's voice recognition expert)

On July 1, 2013, the sixth day of the trial, the prosecutors called Hirotaka Nakasone to testify. He was an FBI expert on voice recognition systems and said that it was impossible to identify anyone's voice from the 2.6 second scream that was heard in the background of the Lauer 911 call before the gunshot blasted into the night.

This author replayed the tape several times and it sounded like a child's voice to her. However, Nakasone's opinion was that only a relative or a person familiar with the screamer's voice could identify it.

Of course, the prosecution had already blown that. While Sybrina Fulton immediately recognized her son's screams, Tracy Martin, the victim's father, declared it wasn't Trayvon contradicting her.

Naturally, O'Mara seized the opportunity to plant the seeds of more doubt in the minds of the jury. The defense team exploited the opportunity created by the prosecutors to have GZ's parents and friends, who all admitted they had never heard him scream before, identify the scream as his even though it made no sense that GZ would have screamed knowing he was armed with a loaded gun.

UNNECESSARY PROSECUTION WITNESS #24:
DORIS SINGLETON
(Sanford police officer)

On July 1, 2013, day six of the trial, the prosecutors called Doris Singleton, the Sanford police officer who interviewed GZ after the shooting. Again, it was a mystery why she was called as a witness because GZ stuck to his story of self-defense and this officer had nothing new to add to the confession that the killer had made to Officer Timothy Smith at the scene.

UNNECESSARY PROSECUTION WITNESS #25:
CHRIS SERINO
(Sanford police investigator)

When Chris Serino was called to testify right after Officer Singleton, he was surly and agitated. He didn't recall the date from the year before when he was transferred for the third time back to the investigation unit. His entire testimony seemed forced and inconsistent. Serino was the only police officer who had initially suggested that GZ might have been guilty of manslaughter for negligently killing Trayvon. Because he was ignored, he seemed bitter and resentful of the prosecutors who were Johnny-come-latelies with a second-degree murder charge.

Why the prosecutors called him as a witness was a closely held secret.

UNNECESSARY PROSECUTION WITNESS #26:
MARK OSTERMAN
(GZ's friend)

There was no reason in the world for the prosecutors to call Mark Osterman, who said GZ was "the best friend I ever had." Putting him on the stand to prove their case was a typical example of the ineptness of these prosecutors and enough reason for Florida to later rise up in outrage and vote Angela Corey out of office. Forever.

If only Sybrina Fulton and Tracy Martin had understood the magnitude of the prosecutors' mistake in calling witnesses like Osterman, they could have mounted a public outcry to petition the governor to replace the prosecutors before the Jury's not guilty verdict.

In Ohio, blunders like this could be grounds for sanctions or disbarment.

UNNECESSARY PROSECUTION WITNESS #27:
DR. VALERIE RAO
(medical examiner, who did not perform Trayvon's autopsy)

On the seventh day of the trial, the prosecutors continued their parade of unnecessary witnesses and called Dr. Valerie Rao. Although she was a Florida state medical examiner, she wasn't the one who had performed the autopsy on Trayvon. That medical examiner was Dr. Shiping Bao, who would be Prosecution Witness #39. , and there were still 11 witnesses ahead of him before the jury would hear his testimony about how Trayvon was killed.

Meanwhile, the prosecutors asked Dr. Rao her expert opinions about GZ's medical records, photos of his alleged injuries caused by Trayvon, and Trayvon's autopsy report. She said that GZ's injuries were "minor" and "very insignificant." In other words, Dr. Rao was another useless witness who merely repeated testimony from earlier witnesses.

UNNECESSARY PROSECUTION WITNESS #28:
KRISTEN BENSON
(fingerprint expert)

On July 2, 2019, the seventh day of the trial, Kristin Benson was the fingerprint expert whose analysis of a latent print from GZ's gun was inconclusive as to whether it came from him or Trayvon during the struggle. Because she had provided no new information, Benson's testimony was a bust.

After sitting through the previous 27 useless witnesses, the jurors were overloaded and in a stupor from too much information.

UNNECESSARY PROSECUTION WITNESS #29:
SONJA BOLES-MELVIN
(GZ's college registrar)

On the eighth day of the trial, Sonja Boles-Melvin was the Seminole State College registrar who identified GZ's college records. It was another bit of useless information that was irrelevant to the prosecution because it didn't add anything to the irrelevant stack of evidence and failed to provide a motive why the volunteer night watchman had killed Trayvon.

UNNECESSARY PROSECUTION WITNESS #30:
LT. SCOTT KEARNS
(Prince William County Police Department)

At last! On the eighth day of the trial, the prosecutors finally called a witness who could provide a motive for why GZ had killed Trayvon. Lieutenant Scott Kearns worked at the Prince William County Police Department where GZ had applied to become a police officer but was rejected. Had he been asked, Kearns could have shed some light on the killer's frustration with the 911 operator when he said, "These assholes always get away!" But once again, the prosecutors dropped the ball and moved on to the next unnecessary witness without asking Kearns the right questions.

UNNECESSARY PROSECUTION WITNESS #31:
CAPTAIN ALEXIS CARTER
(GZ's criminology class professor)

On the eighth day of the trial, the prosecutors once more failed to connect the dots when U.S. Army Captain Alexis Carter testified. He taught GZ's criminology class at Seminole State College and gave him an "A." Prosecutor Richard Mantei fumbled with the direct examination and failed to establish that GZ had premeditatedly used the knowledge of "Stand Your Ground" laws from Carter's class to make his claim of self-defense for killing Trayvon.

Mark O'Mara's defense team was shrewd and didn't object to this witness's irrelevant testimony for two reasons. First, they knew the prosecutors were going to bungle getting anything meaningful out of Carter because they had already blown the direct examinations of the 30 witnesses who had testified before him. And second, because the defense were better lawyers than the prosecutors, on cross-examination they deftly twisted everything Professor Carter said to their own advantage.

UNNECESSARY PROSECUTION WITNESS #32:
JIM KRZENSKI
(Police records clerk)

Following John Guy's opening statement, which lacked the real motive or solid theory about why GZ had shot Trayvon, the prosecutors kept hinting at reasons and hoping the jurors would figure it out for themselves since they couldn't. On the eighth day of the trial, they chased another theory down a blind alley by calling Jim Krzenski. He worked in administrative services for the Sanford Police Department and identified the records from the time that GZ did a ride-along with one of their officers like Kevin Hart did with Ice Cube. The fact that most people would shy away from danger and not place themselves in a police car in harms way proved that GZ had a frustrated fantasy about being a police officer. Still, the prosecutors failed to link his unfulfilled desire to his motive for shooting the unarmed Trayvon.

UNNECESSARY PROSECUTION WITNESS #33:
SCOTT PLEASANTS
(GZ's online course professor)

Plowing ahead with another useless witness on day eight of the trial, the prosecutors called Scott Pleasants. He was the Seminole State College professor from GZ's online class. The killer had switched his goal from becoming a police officer to becoming an attorney and ultimately a prosecutor.

In his front row seat while watching Angela Corey's team behave like rookies, he was probably encouraged that anybody could do the job, even him.

UNNECESSARY PROSECUTION WITNESS #34:
AMY SIEWERT
(Firearms expert who was a crucial witness)

Amy Siewert, the firearms expert, was one of the four witnesses who were necessary for the prosecutors to prove their case.

See Chapter 11, How They Could Have Won.

UNNECESSARY PROSECUTION WITNESS #35:
ANTHONY GORGONE
(DNA expert)

Anthony Gorgone, a DNA analyst from the Florida Department of Law Enforcement, was the last witness to testify before Sybrina Fulton, Trayvon Martin's mother was called to the stand by the prosecutors.

Gorgone was called to disprove GZ's claim that Trayvon had grabbed his gun from the holster on his hip. However, Gorgone said that none of the victim's DNA was found on GZ's pistol or his holster. This supports the conclusion that GZ had lied about it.

Now the ball was in the defense team's hands. Defense counsel Guy West rushed in to shake Gorgone's credibility. While the expert had claimed that fingernail scrapings from Trayvon's hand showed no traces of GZ's DNA, implying that the child had not tried to defend himself before he was shot, the DNA analyst was forced to admit that he didn't know whether all of the teenager's fingernails were scraped or just one. Doubt was cast on his skills as an expert, and the defense scored another victory.

PROSECUTION WITNESS #36 and recalled as #38:
SYBRINA FULTON
(Trayvon's mother, was a crucial witness)

Sybrina Fulton was one of the four witnesses the prosecution needed in order to prove their case. See Chapter 10, How They Could Have Won.

UNNECESSARY PROSECUTION WITNESS #37:
JAHVARIS FULTON
(Trayvon Martin's older brother)

By the time Trayvon's 22-year-old half-brother was called to the stand, Special Prosecutor Angela Corey's team appeared to have given up the fight to get justice for Trayvon and his family. The three prosecutors were listless and just going through the motions of prosecuting his killer when they called Jahvaris to the stand and asked him to identify the screams on the Lauer 911 tape. It was a waste of time since they knew Jahvaris had already told a television reporter he didn't recognize Trayvon's voice.

Because the questions asked on cross-examination are limited to the subjects asked on direct examination, the prosecutors should have avoided the losing issue about who was screaming and confined their questions to telling the jury what Trayvon was like. Unfortunately, Corey's team were not alert and they missed the opportunity for his big brother to share his memories with the six women in the box and show them he was a warm and precious human being who was loved, loving and would forever be sorely missed by his family and friends.

Instead, John Guy opened the door for Jahvaris to be attacked on cross examination. While the prosecutors nodded off and objections like "asked and answered" floated away like sugar plums over their heads, Mark O'Mara battered the 22 year old with the same question until Judge Nelson intervened and put a stop to it. Too bad the damage had already been done and the Jury was doubtful about who was really screaming on the tape.

PROSECUTION WITNESS #39:
SHIPING BAO
(this medical examiner who did perform the autopsy was the last to testify and he was a crucial witness)

Dr. Shiping Bao was one of the four witnesses the prosecution needed to prove their case.

See Chapter 10, How They Could Have Won.

Prosecution Witnesses In the Order They Testified

	Date	Name	Who They Were
1	June 24	**Chad Joseph**	The son of Tracy Martin's fiance
2	June 24	**Andrew Gaugh**	7-Eleven clerk, sold Trayvon the Skittles
3	June 24	**Sean Noffke**	Dispatcher who took GZ's 911 call
4	June 24–25	**Ramona Rumph**	Seminole Co. Sheriff's Office
5	June 25	**Wendy Dorival**	Sanford Police coordinator
6	June 25	**Donald O'Brien**	President of Retreat at Twin Lakes HOA
7	June 25	**Sgt. Anthony Raimondo**	Sanford Police, 2nd officer at the shooting scene
8	June 25	**Diana Smith**	Crime scene technician, Sanford Police
9	June 25	**Selene Bahadoor**	GZ's neighbor, ear witness to the struggle
10	June 26	**Jeanne Manalo**	GZ's neighbor, ear witness to the shooting
11	June 26	**Jayne Syrdyka**	GZ's neighbor, ear witness to the struggle
12	June 26–27	**Rachel Jeantel**	Said she was talking on cell phone with Trayvon
13	June 27	**Raymond MacDonald**	T-Mobile manager brought Trayvon's cell records
14	June 27	**Jenna Lauer**	GZ's neighbor, made the 911 call with screams
15	June 27	**Selma Mora**	GZ's neighbor, testified in Spanish
16	June 28	**Greg McKinney**	Maintained security cameras at Twin Lakes
17	June 28	**Jonathan Good**	GZ's neighbor, saw the struggle
18	June 28	**Jonathan Manalo**	GZ's neighbor aka the good Samaritan took photos of GZ's injuries after the shooting
19	June 28	**Ricardo Ayala**	Sanford Police officer, attempted to revive Trayvon

20	June 28	**Stacey Livingston**	Sanford Fire/EMT
21	June 28	**Timothy Smith**	Sanford Police officer, arrested GZ
22	June 28	**Lindzee Folgate**	Physician assistant, examined GZ's injuries
23	July 1	**Dr. Hirotaka Nakasone**	FBI audio analysis expert
24	July 1	**Doris Singleton**	Sanford Police officer, took GZ's statement
25	July 1–2	**Chris Serino**	Sanford Police detective, case's lead investigator
26	July 2	**Mark Osterman**	Claimed to be GZ's "best friend"
27	July 2	**Dr. Valerie Rao**	Chief medical examiner, Jacksonville, Fla.
28	July 2	**Kristin Benson**	Seminole County Sheriff's Office
29	July 3	**Sonja Bolez-Melvin**	Seminole State College registrar
30	July 3	**Lt. Scott Kearns**	Prince William County, Va. Police Dept.
31	July 3	**Capt. Alexis Carter**	U.S. Army, taught GZ's criminal justice class
32	July 3	**Jim Krzenski**	Sanford Police administrator, ride-along program
33	July 3	**Scott Pleasants**	Seminole State College criminal justice professor
34	July 3	**Amy Siewert**	Firearms expert and FDLE crime lab analyst
35	July 3	**Anthony Gorgone**	FDLE crime lab analyst
36	July 5	**Sybrina Fulton**	Trayvon Martin's mother
37	July 5	**Jahvaris Fulton**	Trayvon Martin's brother
38	July 5	**Sybrina Fulton**	*2nd testimony*
39	July 5	**Dr. Shiping Bao**	Medical examiner, performed Trayvon's autopsy

PART TWO:
MISTAKES PROSECUTORS MADE WITH
THE 19 DEFENSE WITNESSES

If Corey's team did not know the weaknesses in their case that the Defense was eager to exploit, they should have reached out to other litigators to help them to weigh the pros and cons before they made their final list of witnesses for the prosecution. For example, they put Jahvaris Fulton, Trayvon's brother on the stand and then his mother, Sybrina Fulton to identify her son's screams on the Lauer 911 tape. These witnesses opened the door for the defense to counter and cast doubt on their testimony by calling Gladys Zimmerman, the killer's mother, and others including Tracy Martin, the victim's father, to prove that it was not Trayvon who was screaming on the Lauer 911 tape.

Here are more examples of the numerous mistakes the prosecutors made with the defense witnesses:

DEFENSE WITNESS #1: GLADYS ZIMMERMAN
(GZ's mother)

On day nine of the trial, it was the defense's turn, and they showed the prosecutors how to make a great first impression on the jury. Lead Defense Counsel Mark O'Mara left the courtroom and returned with GZ's mother. He escorted her down the aisle to the bailiff and she swore to tell the truth.

The respect O'Mara showed toward Gladys Zimmerman, the mother of a killer, was not lost on the six women in the jury box. The message conveyed was "if you like and believe me, you'll love and believe GZ's mother that her son was a nice boy and would only kill in self-defense."

If the prosecutors had shown such savvy trial tactics during their part of the six-week trial, they might have won.

Mrs. Zimmerman testified emphatically that it was her son screaming in the background of Lauer's call to 911. Yeah, right. GZ was packing heat, namely, a 9 mm Kel-Tec fully loaded semi-automatic pistol with an extra hollow point bullet in the chamber, and he was the one screaming for help. If you buy that, you might be interested in the bridge for sale in the Sahara Desert.

Although they say every mother can hear her baby crying in a room packed with bassinets, it was a stretch for Mrs. Zimmerman to recognize a

second scream—especially when she admitted that she had never heard her son scream like that before. Mrs. Zimmerman was understandably motivated to save her son from a life in prison. At any other time, she probably never would have said that high-pitched squeal of terror had come from her macho son.

Too bad the prosecutors didn't know how to cross-examine this crucial witness for the defense. De Le Rionda was timid and treated GZ's mother with kid gloves. Apparently, he didn't want to offend the six mothers on the jury. However, he should have asked Mrs. Zimmerman whether her son had told her what had happened that night, including whether he was screaming before he shot Trayvon.

Either way, her answer would have been a winner for the prosecution. If GZ had told her he screamed, then she would only be saying it was his scream because he had already told her. And if he hadn't told her he had screamed, that would have cast doubt that it was really hm screaming or he would have told his mother. Furthermore, the prosecutors failed to point out that GZ never mentioned that he had screamed in any of his statements.

Of course, GZ's mother would never have had the chance to testify and earn the jury's sympathy if the prosecutors hadn't introduced the Lauer 911 call into evidence in the first place. It wasn't necessary to prove their prima facie case of how and why Trayvon Martin was slain. Angela Corey's team should not have veered off into contested matters like who was screaming that were fodder for the defense. They should have limited their witnesses to proving the five elements of second-degree murder. Then they should have rested their case and sat down.

The burden would have then shifted to GZ to convince the jury he had killed Trayvon in self-defense. However, there was no way O'Mara would have exposed his client to a life sentence for second-degree murder. In light of the contradictions in the defendant's video statements, the defense would never have let GZ get on the stand to testify and would have pleaded him out to manslaughter.

DEFENSE WITNESS #2: JORGE MESA
(GZ's uncle)

Unlike the prosecutors, who were arrogant, ignorant, or just didn't care to curry sympathy from the jurors, the defense front loaded their case with GZ's family. They sent the message that the killer was a nice but cowardly fellow who got scared in a fight with a teenager who weighed 60 pounds less than he did.

The prosecutors failed to drive the point home with the jury that it made no sense for GZ to scream since he had a fully loaded weapon on his hip and had pursued Trayvon in a rage after calling 911.

DEFENSE WITNESS #3: SANDRA OSTERMAN
(GZ's friend)

On July 8, 2013, day 10 of the trial, Sondra Osterman, the wife of prosecution witness Mark Osterman, gave a glowing description of GZ. The Ostermans claimed to have written a book (that this author was unable to find) and planned to donate the profits to the killer. So why didn't the prosecutors hammer her greedy motive during Sondra's cross-examination? Furthermore, since both Ostermans were solidly on GZ's side, why did the prosecutors call Mark as their witness to prove the second-degree murder case against their good friend?

DEFENSE WITNESS #4: GERI RUSSO
(GZ's coworker)

Geri Russo testified on July 8, 2019. Russo was Zimmerman's coworker at mortgage company Digital Risk. While there was a connection between the first three defense witnesses because they were relatives and arguably familiar with GZ's voice in various circumstances, Russo's testimony was more likely a character reference. And while it appeared that the defense had called her to identify GZ's 2.6 second scream on the Lauer 911 tape, the sly O'Mara steered her into complimenting GZ's character and saying that the killer was a reliable worker.

Meanwhile, the prosecutors decided not to object. When Russo stated that she had never heard GZ yell or scream before, the prosecutors should have leapt to their feet to strike her entire testimony as lacking a foundation and booted her off the stand.

DEFENSE WITNESS #5: MARK OSTERMAN
(GZ's friend)

It was ridiculous that Mark Osterman was a witness for the prosecution during the second week of the trial and then got back on the stand on July 8, 2013 and testified for the defense. Osterman was the husband of Sondra Osterman, who also testified for the defense a few hours before her husband. Both were GZ's good friends, and Mark said that he had taught GZ how to shoot. How many lessons did it take to pull the trigger of a semi- automatic weapon on a child who was just several inches away?

DEFENSE WITNESS #6: LEEANNE BENJAMIN
(GZ's friend)

On July 8, 2013, under the pretext of identifying GZ's screams on the Lauer 911 tape, the slick defense team continued its march of character witnesses. Their real purpose was to show the jury that GZ was a nice guy. Ordinarily, character witnesses are not allowed to testify when a defendant doesn't take the stand. However, these inept prosecutors weren't familiar with the rules of criminal procedure.

What was lost in Leeanne Benjamin's testimony and those of the other defense witnesses was that GZ was unstable. He couldn't hold a job and flitted from working at a mortgage company to selling insurance but never found anything he was good at. Then he discovered that he was good at shooting an unarmed boy at close range.

DEFENSE WITNESS #7: JOHN DONNELLY
(GZ's friend)

John Donnelly and Leanne Benjamin were another husband and wife duo who swore that GZ was as normal as apple pie. Although neither of them, nor any of the other witnesses the prosecutors sat comatose through, had ever heard GZ yell or scream, they were all certain it was his voice on the Lauer 911 tape wailing like a terrified child.

Donnelly said he trusted GZ and believed in his innocence so much he took him to the store and outfitted him with suits and ties for his court appearances. How odd was that to do even for your favorite relative accused of murder? Regardless, this curious behavior was not challenged by the prosecutors.

While Donnelly claimed GZ was a sharp guy, why wasn't he rich enough to buy his own clothes? Why didn't GZ have his own money? A normal American guy would have been too proud to let another man dress him up like a Ken doll. Was this an act of kindness or was Donnelly motivated by something else, like giving him a reward for killing a black kid? Donnelly said that he had had many conversations with GZ. If this were true, he would have known GZ's opinions about guns and race. GZ didn't have to hate blacks to kill one if in his heart he believed they weren't equal to whites and therefore, were disposable.

Even more unbelievable than buying another man clothes for no good reason, Donnelly claimed to be a Vietnam War veteran who had picked up the skill of distinguishing screaming voices above the din of gunfire in combat. More likely, Donnelly was an interrogator who could have gotten his kicks peeking into doorways while his comrades tortured prisoners.

DEFENSE WITNESS #8 and recalled as #10: DORIS SINGLETON
(Sanford police officer)

Doris Singleton was initially called as Witness #24 for the prosecution. Although she had conducted the first interview at the police station when GZ arrived in handcuffs, she had nothing new or significant to report to move the case forward. Then, on July 10, 2013, Singleton was called back to the stand by the defense to confirm that the killer did not know that Trayvon had died until she told him. That was impossible.

GZ knew the wound he inflicted on Trayvon was fatal because he shot him at close range through the chest with a bullet that imploded on impact, destroying muscle and bones. The killer made no effort to help the boy and stood around for a few minutes while Trayvon bled out in the grass. Although the neighborhood watchman made his second call that night to 911, he apparently got cold feet and didn't mention he had shot a guy. It's reasonable to assume that GZ withheld that crucial information because he didn't want the dispatcher to send an ambulance in case by some miracle the teenager could be saved and tell what really happened. Unfortunately, the prosecutors failed to ask about this on cross-examination of Singleton or any other witness.

What's more, the prosecutors missed a crucial fact that could have turned their case around. Since GZ told Officer Singleton that he was carrying a flashlight, why didn't he use it to defend himself instead of his semi-automatic Kel-Tec with the lethal bullets? One bash on Trayvon's head would have been enough of a deterrent to send him running off into the night and given GZ time to get back to his car.

Once more, these prosecutors failed to dig deeper and completely ignored other glaring evidence that could have shredded GZ's claim of self- defense.

DEFENSE WITNESS #9: CHRIS SERINO
(Sanford police lead investigator)

On Day 10, Sanford Police Lead Investigator Chris Serino testified for the second time when he was recalled to the stand by the defense. But they didn't have to bother, because on Day 6, as a witness for the prosecution, Serino had already done a good job undercutting their case.

DEFENSE WITNESS #11: ADAM POLLOCK
(Gym owner and GZ's MMA instructor)

On day 13 of the trial, July 8, 2013, Adam Pollock testified for the defense. He owned the gym where GZ took lessons on mixed martial arts (MMA).

He said that GZ was untrainable and that on a scale of five, he was a one in terms of his skills. The implication was that the 200-pound man couldn't defend himself against Trayvon, a 17-year-old boy who weighed 60 pounds less than him.

In ordinary circumstances where prosecutors would have been competent, this witness would not have been allowed to tell the jury about GZ's failure to learn how to fight. Because GZ didn't testify, this line of questions was irrelevant and lacked a foundation. However, Corey's team had allowed their own witnesses to talk about GZ's skills and, once again, were hanging from their own rope.

Still, all was not lost. On cross-examination, the prosecutors could have asked whether Pollock knew for certain whether GZ was faking being a wuss. It was possible that pretending to be helpless was part of a premeditated scheme to get away with murder. No one knew how long GZ could have been planning to scare his wife into staying with him. But the prosecutors didn't even try to shake Pollock's testimony with obvious questions. They lacked the courage of their convictions because they had no convictions. The case was just blowing in the wind.

"Wake up, prosecutors! Wake up!" I often shouted at the television screen. Alas, they didn't hear me.

DEFENSE WITNESS #12: TRACY MARTIN
(Trayvon's father)

On day 13, the defense brought Tracy Martin to the stand to let the jury see him squirm as he tried to explain away his earlier statement that it wasn't his son screaming in the background on the Lauer 911 tape. Instead of saying that his pride had kept him from identifying his son's voice because he didn't want his son to be remembered as weak, Tracy hemmed and hawed. Of course, the jury didn't buy his new story.

If the prosecutors hadn't made the mistake of putting the Lauer 911 tape into evidence for Sybrina Fulton to identify the screams, there would have been nothing for him to contradict.

DEFENSE WITNESS #13: BILL LEE
(Fired Sanford police chief)

When Bill Lee, the former Sanford police chief, was called by the defense to testify on Day 14 of the trial, he wreaked of bitterness. He was kept out of the room when all the 911 calls were played for the family, and then he was fired for refusing to file charges against GZ. As a result, Lee insisted there wasn't enough evidence to arrest GZ for any crime.

Naturally, the prosecutors failed to shake Lee's testimony during cross-examination. If the police were against you in a criminal trial, you are screwed. The prosecutors should have filed a motion in limine to exclude Lee's testimony for the defense because it was irrelevant that they didn't initially charge GZ.

Of course, Lee would never have been called to testify if the prosecutors had done what they were supposed to do and limited their case to the 4 witnesses who could have proved that GZ was guilty of second-degree murder.

DEFENSE WITNESS #14: VINCENT DI MAIO
(Forensic pathologist)

On July 9, 2013, Vincent Di Maio, a forensic pathologist, testified that Trayvon's hoodie was not properly preserved. It couldn't be used for evidence because it was stored in a plastic bag and became moldy. Then Di Maio delivered the zinger that became the central argument in the defense's case: He said that Trayvon was on top of GZ when he was shot.

On cross-examination, the prosecutors failed to rise to the challenge to make the point that who was on top was irrelevant. This is because during a struggle, especially on the ground where fighters usually swap positions, GZ could have purposefully rolled his victim on top.

If you planned to use self-defense for killing somebody in a fight you started, wouldn't it be easier to convince your audience that your victim was on top when you shot him? It makes sense that the screaming before the shot rang out was a terrified Trayvon when he felt a gun stuck in his ribs.

DEFENSE WITNESS #15: NORTON BONAPARTE
(Sanford city manager)

Norton Bonaparte, the Sanford city manager, played the Lauer 911 call for Trayvon's parents. The defense called Bonaparte to the stand to show the jury that Tracy's first reaction was that it wasn't his son screaming. Later on, the father tried to change his story to be consistent with his former wife's identification of their son's voice and got tripped up for lying.

Like the fake issue of who was on top, who was screaming on the tape was a red herring. It should have been indisputable that a man with a loaded pistol on his hip would be scared, much less scream for his life.

DEFENSE WITNESS #16: ELOISE DILLIGARD
(GZ's neighbor)

Eloise Dilligard, a black woman, testified from her sick bed. Her face was projected on a screen in the courtroom to indicate to the jury that GZ didn't hate blacks. Confused because GZ took a black girl to his prom, the prosecutors avoided the controversy of whether he was a racist. Meanwhile, the defense paraded black lawyers and assistants around the courtroom and called witnesses to prove that he wasn't a racist.

Just because a white person has a black friend or two doesn't prove he's not a racist. GZ could still have selected Trayvon to be his victim because it was easier to get away with killing a black person in Florida.

DEFENSE WITNESS #17: DENNIS ROOT
(Law enforcement expert)

On July 10, 2013, it was baffling when Dennis Root testified as an expert in law enforcement specializing in self-defense and "Stand Your Ground." Root's opinions were irrelevant and within the purview of the jury to decide. Once more, the prosecutors sat on their hands like first-year law students. Instead of moving to strike his testimony, they asked Root more questions on cross-examination that allowed the defense to redirect and delve even further into his biased and irrelevant opinions.

While Prosecutor John Guy tossed around big words like "continuum" to impress them, the jurors yawned and were impatient for the trial to be over.

DEFENSE WITNESS #18: OLIVIA BERTALAN
(GZ's former neighbor)

On July 10, 2013, Olivia Bertalan was called to testify for the defense. Once more, the prosecutors allowed a witness who was irrelevant to the killing of Trayvon Martin to say things that hurt their case. Bertalan wasn't even on the premises at the time of the shooting because she had moved from The Retreat at Twin Lakes following a burglary at her condo.

The prosecutors should have filed a motion in limine to persuade Judge Nelson that Bertalan's testimony was inflammatory and outweighed its probative value. What that means is if evidence can provoke the emotions of the jury and is not essential to prove or disprove any element of a crime, it should be excluded. The prosecution was trying to use Bertalan's fear of being robbed to justify that GZ had chased and killed Trayvon. It inflamed the jury against the teenager, and because she knew nothing about what had happened that night in Sanford, her testimony should have been excluded.

DEFENSE WITNESS #19: ROBERT ZIMMERMAN, SR.
(GZ's father)

He who talks last talks loudest. In a shrewd move, the last witness the defense called before the six lady jurors was GZ's father, Robert Zimmerman, Sr., a Southern white man. He testified that it was most definitely his son screaming in the background on the Lauer 911 call.

What else would you expect him to say? He was trying to save his son's life. And Mr. Zimmerman probably believed GZ's story that he shot Trayvon in self-defense despite the hollow point bullets that implied a malicious intent to kill him. Again, the prosecutors dropped the ball and should have prevented GZ's father from testifying since his son chose to remain silent and didn't testify.

Defense Witnesses In The Order They Testified

	Date	Name	Who They Are
1	July 5	**Gladys Zimmerman**	George Zimmerman's mother
2	July 5	**Jorge Mesa**	George Zimmerman's uncle (Gladys' brother)
3	July 8	**Sondra Osterman**	Friend of Zimmerman, Mark Osterman's wife
4	July 8	**Mark Osterman**	*2nd testimony*
5	July 8	**Geri Russo**	Friend, former co-worker of Zimmerman
6	July 8	**Leanne Benjamin**	Friend, former business associate of Zimmerman
7	July 8	**John Donnelly**	Friend of Zimmerman, husband of Leanne Benjamin
8	July 8	**Doris Singleton**	*2nd testimony*
9	July 8	**Chris Serino**	*2nd testimony*
10	July 8	**Doris Singleton**	*3rd testimony*
11	July 8	**Adam Pollock**	Gym owner, trained Zimmerman in MMA fighting
12	July 8	**Tracy Martin**	Trayvon Martin's father
13	July 8	**Bill Lee**	Former Sanford Police chief
14	July 9	**Dr. Vincent Di Maio**	Forensic pathologist, gunshot wound expert
15	July 9	**Norton Bonaparte**	Sanford city manager
16	July 9	**Eloise Dilligard**	Former neighbor of Zimmerman
17	July 10	**Dennis Root**	Law enforcement trainer, private investigator
18	July 10	**Olivia Bertalan**	Former neighbor
19	July 10	**Robert Zimmerman Sr.**	George Zimmerman's father

Prosecution's Rebuttal Witness

	Date	Name	Who They Are
1	July 10	**Adam Pollock**	GZ's martial arts instructor, second testimony, was Defense witness #11

PART THREE:
THE BIGGEST PROSECUTOR MISTAKES

Special Prosecutor Angela Corey said she charged GZ with the right crime, second-degree murder, and that the not guilty verdict was a complete surprise to them.

It's impossible that these prosecutors handled GZ's trial like rank amateurs and broke all 12 rules set forth in this book for winning but didn't know it. It's impossible that the prosecutors had 95 years of criminal trial experience among them but didn't know it was forbidden to curse at the jury during an opening statement. Add to that a thousand more mistakes, and there was no way they were clueless about their poor performance.

And yet, while on television discussing the confessed killer's acquittal, these prosecutors brazenly denied that they could have done anything different to convict GZ. I cringed watching them whining and shifting the blame to Florida's "Stand Your Ground" law. And worse, they pointed the finger at Rachel Jeantel, who never should have been called to testify in the first place. Not even a newbie lawyer would have taken the risk of calling an unprepared and emotional witness like Jeantel to prove essential elements of their case.

These and many other poor choices doomed the prosecutors from the start. Here are the biggest mistakes that did them in.

BIGGEST TRIAL MISTAKE #1:
John Guy delivered the opening statement from hell

Prosecutor John Guy broke Rule #8, "Charm and Never Curse at the Jury." In his opening statement he blurted out, "F----ing a--holes! They always get away!" Of course, the six women on the jury were offended. From then on, every word Guy spoke was annoying and made them frown. Defying logic, the prosecution brought the brash prosecutor back to question their first witness. While he asked questions during direct examination, the jury shot daggers at him.

BIGGEST TRIAL MISTAKE #2:

They failed to force GZ to testify

The prosecutors had the burden of proving the defendant guilty beyond a reasonable doubt. However, when GZ claimed self-defense, the burden shifted to him to prove it beyond a reasonable doubt. The only way he could have done that was to testify in front of the jury.

Instead of forcing him to get on the stand to tell his version of what happened so they could attack any lies and inconsistencies, the prosecutors showed the neighborhood watchman's three video statements to the six women who would decide his fate. It is well-settled that a picture is worth a thousand words and GZ had practiced looking and sounding sincere. As the jurors saw his images over and over again, reasonable doubt crept into their minds. Letting GZ off the like that was a strategy that didn't speak well for the prosecutors' combined 95 years of criminal trial experience.

If they had followed tried and true trial tactics by forcing GZ to testify, Lead Defense Counsel Mark O'Mara would have pleaded GZ out to manslaughter rather than allow his client to risk a longer prison term for second-degree murder. The misguided choices continually made by Corey's team from start to finish during the trial will always baffle this author and prosecutors around the nation.

BIGGEST TRIAL MISTAKE #3:

They showed GZ's three video statements to the jury

Harry Houdini would put on a straight-jacket and allow chains to be wrapped around his body and secured with a padlock. Upside down, the magician would be lowered into an icy river where he would escape and swim to the surface. Too bad this magician wasn't around to help the prosecutors escape from the shackles they put on their case by showing GZ's three self-serving video statements to the jury.

Were they stupid, determined to lose, or just didn't give a damn? It was immensely frustrating to watch Corey's team try to contradict the lies and inconsistencies in GZ's video statements. If they hadn't used them as evidence in the first place, they could have easily won the case.

While the prosecutors wasted the entire trial chasing their tails in a maze they had created. Had they forced GZ to get on the stand and tell his story, they could have destroyed it. For example, GZ claimed that Trayvon was menacing because the teenager had circled his car and stared at him.

However, the teen was simply curious to find out who was following him. After all, it was his father's neighborhood and it could have been one of Tracy Martin's friends. When Trayvon got a good look at the stranger, he realized he was no friend and took off running. It must have been something in GZ's cold eyes that had frightened him.

While viewing GZ's videos where he admitted he chased Trayvon down, the prosecutors should have been outraged and gotten to work on the killer's cross-examination. Instead, somebody on Corey's team got the bright idea to use GZ's video statements to prove the state's own case.

Whose side were these prosecutors on?

BIGGEST TRIAL MISTAKE #4:
They didn't bring Trayvon back to life in the courtroom

One of the most glaring mistakes in GZ's trial was the failure to tell the story of Trayvon's life to the jury. In a surprising lack of insight for how to persuade jurors the prosecutors didn't bring Sybrina and Tracy's son back alive through photos, videos, and stories told by his loved ones, especially his mother, to bring tears to the eyes of the six women who held the killer's fate in their hands.

Instead of showing Trayvon as a happy and loving child, brother, and high schooler, whose goals and dreams would never be fulfilled, the prosecutors shied away in fear of exposing his faults. Nobody's perfect.

And no matter what rules he broke or pranks he was involved with, these so-called seasoned prosecutors should have focused on his life which was cut short depriving him of the milestones of growing up and denying Trayvon his full potential as a human being to make contributions to our society.

BIGGEST TRIAL MISTAKE #5:

The prosecutors let the defense portray Trayvon as the incredible hulk with four arms

The prosecutors blew their own case by showing GZ's video statements unchallenged by cross-examination. It was unwise to help the defense tell GZ's fabricated story to the jury. A prime example, the killer said that Trayvon had covered his mouth to silence his screams while at the same time held down his shoulders to prevent him from fighting back while also bashing his head on the sidewalk three dozen times!

This was a tale straight out of Hollywood or GZ's overripe imagination. For it was impossible for a 140-pound boy to pin GZ, who weighed a whopping 200 pounds, while he was fighting for his life.

Remember, the syndrome of "flight or fight?" GZ's adrenalin would have coursed through his body and made him even stronger to save himself.

BIGGEST TRIAL MISTAKE #6:

They failed to discredit GZ's story that Trayvon bashed his head on the sidewalk 30 times

GZ claimed that he shot Trayvon to save his own life because the teenager had bashed his head more than 30 times on the sidewalk. The facts prove otherwise. Every earwitness and eyewitness placed the final struggle on the grass, and that's where the police found Trayvon's body. By his own admission during his statement at the police station, the killer said he never touched the teen after he collapsed on the grass.

Despite this overwhelming evidence that disproves GZ's claim of having killed Trayvon in self-defense, the prosecutors failed during their opening statement, closing arguments, and every other opportunity to hammer home that GZ had fired the shot during the final struggle on the grass and his life was not at stake when he killed Trayvon. To support a claim of self-defense, the law required the threat to be real and immediate. In this instance it was neither.

Further proof was if Trayvon had banged GZ's head on the concrete sidewalk thirty times, GZ would have serious injuries to his scalp and would have had a concussion. On the contrary, the killer had minor scrapes, was alert and never lost consciousness. Immediately after the shooting, witnesses saw him strolling about. The photos taken by Jonathan Manola revealed that GZ was bright eyed and vigilant. When he was taken to the police station GZ never complained of a headache and gave no indication that he felt ill or was in pain.

The confessed killer refused to go the ER to get checked out with a CAT scan or MRI of his brain because he knew Trayvon did nothing to hurt him.

BIGGEST TRIAL MISTAKE #7:
GZ had let Trayvon die and the prosecutors missed it

The prosecutors were so preoccupied with trying to discredit GZ's video statements that they missed crucial evidence that showed the killer's depraved indifference to human life, an element they needed to prove he committed second-degree murder. In his first video filmed at the police station, GZ said he didn't know that Trayvon had died. It was an obvious lie not only because he had used the deadly hollow-point bullet, but after he shot the boy, he said Trayvon didn't stand up or move.

GZ didn't try to help his victim, and worse, at 7:20 p.m., three minutes after the fatal shot blasted into the night, the killer called 911 for the second time. However, GZ merely repeated his earlier call about an intruder and failed to mention that he had shot Trayvon. He didn't bother to summon help while Sybrina Fulton's child bled out in the grass.

Perhaps, GZ didn't want to take the chance that the paramedics would save Trayvon and he would tell them what really happened. And so, when Jonathan Manola came out of his condo and offered to call 911, GZ replied that he had already called them. The killer deliberately misled Manola into believing help was on the way. And yet, during the trial there was not a single mention by the prosecutors of GZ's cold-blooded scheme to deprive Trayvon of prompt medical assistance, regardless of the fact that one of the elements of second-degree murder is a depraved indifference to human life.

BIGGEST TRIAL MISTAKE #8:

*The prosecutors lost the chance to prove it was Trayvon screaming
on the Lauer 911 tape*

Before GZ's trial started, the prosecutors lost their chance to prove it
was Trayvon who was screaming on Lauer's 911 tape. At the Sanford
police station, when the tape was played for the family, Tracy Martin was
emphatic that he didn't recognize Trayvon's voice. No matter that GZ had
said he didn't recognize his own voice doing the screaming, the victim's
own father made the question of who was screaming moot. It was useless
when the prosecutors tried to identify Trayvon's voice by putting Sybrina
Fulton on the stand.

It was understandable that initially Tracy didn't want to recognize the
screams because he didn't want his son to be known as a coward. He
realized too late how important it was to establish that Trayvon was crying
for help. Unfortunately, he had opened the door for defense witnesses to
testify that it was GZ who was screaming. When the Defense also called
Trayvon's father to the stand, it was useless when he tried to backtrack and
claim it was his son after all.

Showing no shame, Mr. and Mrs. Zimmerman and several of the
killer's friends, marched to the stand and swore it was GZ's voice on the
911 tape. Really? It defied common sense that GZ would scream at all
when he knew his loaded semi-automatic weapon was on his hip within
easy reach.

BIGGEST TRIAL MISTAKE #9:

*The prosecutors failed to prevent the defense re-enactment of the
crime film from being shown to the jury*

When Judge Nelson allowed the defense to show the animated film
showing GZ's version of the confrontation and why he killed Trayvon that
night, she violated the hearsay rule and the basic rule that every piece of
evidence is required to have the proper foundation. That means it can't be
shown to the jury unless it has been authenticated as genuine by the person
who saw and heard everything portrayed in the film.

The key to America's judicial system is for parties to bring their
witnesses and other proof into open court where they can be subjected to

cross-examination under the watchful eyes of the jury. It's not supposed to be a free-for-all. The "hearsay rule" excludes evidence that was said out of court. "Said" includes everything spoken out loud, written, drawn, or recorded with or without sound, including moving pictures and animation.

There are a few exceptions to the hearsay rule that allow what was said out of court to be used as evidence. For example, the last words of someone dying can be quoted in court if that person was talking about who killed them. It is assumed that most people would not go to meet their maker with a lie on their lips.

Since GZ didn't testify and the producer of the animation had no personal knowledge of the facts, the film was hearsay and it lacked a proper foundation. The hearsay rule prohibits anything to be told to the jury if it was not said in open court and under oath. Regardless, the prosecutors left their brains at home and didn't make the appropriate objections to the defense animation being shown to the jury during closing arguments or ever.

Could it be that Corey's team didn't know or understand the rules of evidence? In Florida, there was no exception to the hearsay rule that would have allowed the defense animation into evidence. By allowing it to be shown to the jury, Judge Nelson made a prejudicial and insurmountable error against the prosecution.

Although the animated re-enactment of how CZ had killed Trayvon was produced under the direction of the defense team, it was also not the defense counsel's story either because they were not present at the scene of the killing. And because GZ did not get on the stand and subject himself to cross-examination, the animation was never authenticated under the rules of evidence and therefore, it lacked the proper foundation.

One picture being worth a thousand words, GZ's version of what happened that night was imprinted on the minds of the six women who sat in the box as they watched the reenactment of the crime where the roles were switched to make Trayvon the aggressor and GZ the victim.

What's more, the prosecution knew about the animation early enough to make a film of their own. Why didn't they?

Unfortunately, the State has no right to appeal a not guilty verdict.

BIGGEST TRIAL MISTAKE #10:

The prosecutors failed to make a list of what they had to prove and to check it twice

Things can get hectic in the middle of a trial. The best way for a prosecutor or other litigator to keep track of the evidence and points they have made is to make a list. As it progresses, they should check it off and then check it again before resting their case.

Unfortunately, it was obvious that the prosecutors did not make a list.

They were lost and showed that they didn't have a clue how to win and convict GZ of second-degree murder.

BIGGEST TRIAL MISTAKE #11:

The prosecutors brought a dummy into the court room and the defense beat their case up with it

The dummy I'm referring to at this time was not the prosecutors but the foam life-sized dummy that some idiot, possibly to save the cost of making a video, convinced the prosecution would be useful for reenacting the crime in front of the jury. Only it backfired. When Mark O'Mara sat astride it and started smacking it, I burst out laughing.

There had to be some chuckles among the jurors too. The dummy was supposed to portray GZ, but the prosecutors failed to anticipate what a clever defense counsel would do with it. They should have first tried it out on a kid to find out its potential ridiculousness before O'Mara made fools of them in open court.

Rather than bring life-sized manikins with the heights and weights of the killer and his victim, the prosecutors brought a 20-pound dummy made of foam to represent GZ in the deadly struggle. No dummy himself, Mark O-Mara got astride and beat its brains out. In the process he persuaded the jury that it was not only possible, but easy, for a scrawny teenager to hold down a big man like GZ.

I did an experiment with a friend with the same disparity in weight. I, at 140 pounds, took Trayvon's place on top, while he, at 200 pounds, lay on the bottom. He easily pushed me off with less motivation to do so than GZ, who claimed his life was at stake.

It didn't make sense that a man of any size who was truly terrified and fighting for his life would just lie there and not fight back. GZ's adrenalin had to be pumping from the second he got out of his car and started chasing Trayvon with a pistol hidden under his jacket. And yet, the ladies on the jury bought the defense's story that skinny Trayvon had attacked the 200 pound man who was too cowardly to fight back.

If a man were on the jury, he never would have fallen for that one.

BIGGEST TRIAL MISTAKE #12:
They called Trayvon's mother too late to get the jury's sympathy

Ever since they first sat down in the box, the jury was anticipating hearing the victim's story from his mother. Tissues at the ready, they anticipated every horrible detail of her loss. Incredibly, Sybrina Fulton was Witness #36 and by the time she got on the stand, the trial was almost over and the jurors had all but forgotten about her ordeal.

Making it worse, Trayvon's mother was dry-eyed and stoic. Of all the witnesses, Sybrina appeared to have been coached by the prosecutors to control her emotions. Instead of crying and talking about "my son," she was cool and detached, referring to the boy she had given birth to as "Trayvon Martin" instead of "my baby." Hey, prosecutors, you dropped the ball! This mother's moment was supposed to be passionate and break the jury's hearts.

By contrast, the defense got it right by calling GZ's mother as their first witness to humanize the child killer.

BIGGEST TRIAL MISTAKE #13:
The arresting officer was also called too late

Witness #21 was Timothy Smith, the Sanford police officer who was the first to arrive on the scene after Trayvon was shot on February 26, 2012. He was the one who heard GZ's confession and arrested him. How absurd was it that the arresting officer wasn't called until Day 4 of the trial?

Rather than calling the most important witnesses to tell their stories and make the greatest impact on the jury, the other witnesses for the prosecution testified in a mindless chronological order of how the events had occurred that night in Sanford.

BIGGEST TRIAL MISTAKE #14:

The prosecutors failed to make timely "asked and answered!" Objections when the defense cross-examined weapon's expert Amy Siewert

During cross-examination, Amy Siewert had already answered twice that her tests had determined that GZ's pistol was working properly. While O'Mara kept pausing to allow the apathy at Bernie De La Rionda's table to sink into the minds of the jurors, the prosecutor's silence on behalf of poor Trayvon was deafening.

Corey's team should have been on their feet with "Objection! Asked and answered!" But no. The prosecutors, who otherwise strutted around the courtroom running their mouths about inconsequential matters, shirked their duty to speak out.

> **O'Mara:** "It was not malfunctioning in any form?"
> **Amy Siewert:** "No. There were no indications that anything on this pistol was malfunctioning."

If the firearms expert had been properly prepped by the prosecutors, she would have blurted out, "But it was the defendant who malfunctioned!"

BIGGEST TRIAL MISTAKE #15:

The prosecutors failed to have an expert on African-American speech prove Trayvon never would have told GZ "You're going to die tonight, motherf----r!"

Trayvon Martin got good grades, ran errands for his grandma and was probably a lot like Theo Huxtable. However, one of his friends was Rachel Jeantel who was from the hood. It was likely that he had spent time texting with her because her attitude and slang were more exciting than the humdrum speech of most kids at his school. And like most teenagers, when he expressed his feelings to people other than his parents, Trayvon tried to sound cool.

As a result, he would never have spoken in proper sentences like "You're going to die tonight." Experts on "black slang," aka African American English, should have been called to dispute that black youth talked the way GZ said Trayvon did during the struggle. No hip young person would ever have uttered the stiff, "You're going to die tonight." Although GZ had tacked on "motherf----r" to add ghetto realism, it still didn't ring true. Remember, Judge Judy said if something doesn't make sense, don't believe it.

Trayvon had shown the good sense to run from what he saw in the dark was a white man chasing him in the Deep South. This proved that the teenager had no intentions to harm GZ. However, once he was cornered and attacked, a ghetto child probably would have said, "I'm gonna f--k you up!" instead of "You're going to die".

BIGGEST TRIAL MISTAKE #16:
The prosecutors failed to have an expert on African-American speech dispute Trayvon's last words were "you got me!"

Trayvon had to feel the warm and sticky blood oozing out of his chest and knew that the "creepy ass cracker" had dealt him a serious injury. More likely, his last words were either, "Why did you shoot me?" or "Mama!"

But for the tragedy, this author would have laughed out loud when GZ claimed that Trayvon's last words were "You got me!" Those words were from the killer's own childhood memory of Western movies, not the exclamation of a mortally wounded black teenager in modern times. More likely, GZ had flipped the script and said, "I got you, motherf----r!"

BIGGEST TRIAL MISTAKE #17:
The prosecutors failed to disprove GZ's story that Trayvon jumped out of the bushes that weren't there

In each of his three video statements that were inexplicably used as evidence by the prosecutors, GZ repeated his claim that he was walking along the sidewalk when Trayvon jumped out of the bushes and attacked him. The problem was that there were no bushes to jump out of at the intersection where the confrontation began!

The photos of the crime scene were projected on a large screen for the jury and revealed that the bushes were yards away up close to the building. While watching the trial, this author pointed at the clear space between the sidewalk and the bushes and yelled, "Look! There are no bushes there for him to jump out of!"

Unfortunately, the prosecutors didn't hear my efforts to help them.

BIGGEST TRIAL MISTAKE #18:
The prosecutors missed GZ's obvious threat to his wife

While Trayvon lay dying in the grass, the good Samaritan came out to take pictures of GZ's scrapes and bruises. Then he offered to call the killer's wife on his own cell phone. When he asked what GZ wanted him to say, the response was "Tell her I shot someone."

That wasn't a normal message from a husband concerned about his wife's reaction. To avoid panicking and shocking her, a man who loved his wife would have softened the blow with "Tell her something happened but I'm okay." Or he would have said, "Tell her I'm okay but meet me at the police station."

It was another curious thing that GZ didn't ask his wife to bring a lawyer. That's how sure he was he would get away with it.

In this author's scenario that GZ had set out to find a quarry to kill as a warning to his wife and make her come back home to him, he had months to plan what he would do and say. From his criminal law class, GZ would have picked up helpful tips for his diabolical scheme.

It's very suspicious that the killer confronted Trayvon Martin directly behind Jonathon Manola's condo. Having this "Good Samaritan" come out right after hearing the gun blast to take impromptu pictures of GZ's injuries was too convenient to be a mere coincidence. While the life drained out of a child, they hung around talking. What about?

Furthermore, if GZ had truly been interested in what Trayvon was up to and had not planned to execute him, why didn't he confront the boy in the street during his first call to 911? GZ told the operator that the kid was coming right at his car. With a witness on the phone and knowing these calls were recorded, wasn't that the perfect time to ask Trayvon what he was doing in the neighborhood instead of chasing after him?

BIGGEST TRIAL MISTAKE #19:
The prosecutors failed to produce their own re-enactment of the crime

Based on GZ's statements, the defense produced an animated re-enactment of how the crime occurred that Judge Nelson let them show to the jury during closing arguments. It's a mystery why the prosecutors didn't take advantage of their opportunity to show their own film to prove GZ was the aggressor. They put on their case first and could have impressed the jury before the defense could have contradicted it with their own film.

So, why didn't the prosecutors make their own re-enactment?

BIGGEST TRIAL MISTAKE #20:
They let the jury hear GZ blame God for killing Trayvon

GZ blamed God for killing Trayvon Martin during one of his video statements. He said, "It was God's will." To any Christian, it was blasphemy. Also, it was proof of the fifth element of second-degree murder, namely, that GZ had killed Trayvon with a depraved disregard for human life.

However, the prosecutors weren't smart enough to see that attributing his evil deed to God proved GZ's lack of remorse for taking the life of a teenager who merely went out to buy a bag of Skittles.

BIGGEST TRIAL MISTAKE #21:
The prosecutors focused on GZ instead of telling Trayvon Martin's story

The victim's story must be the focus of the prosecutor's case. Through the eyes of the people who loved him, the jury must know where he lived, how he played, and what his dreams were. They must hear about the wonderful things that he did for his friends and family and learn that he was irreplaceable.

And yet, these prosecutors failed to portray Trayvon's life and what losing him meant to his family. While they showed GZ's self-serving video statements, there was not a single audio or visual display of Sybrina Fulton's child living, breathing, and laughing. We learned from the media that Trayvon was suspended from school for painting graffiti on a wall, not for fighting or stealing. He was a good kid who took the time to help out his grandparents. But the prosecutors made sure that the jury never got to see or hear the victim's story. Why not?

BIGGEST TRIAL MISTAKE #22:
The prosecutors called too many witnesses

The GZ prosecutors should have simplified their case. Instead, they overwhelmed the jury with every piece of evidence they could find and trotted 38 witnesses to the stand. What each was supposed to contribute to prove that GZ was guilty of shooting Trayvon with a depraved mind and disregard for human life got lost in the parade.

The best and usual way for a prosecutor to keep control of the progress of a case is to make a list of the major points each witness was intended to prove then check them off as they testified. Unfortunately, it was obvious that the prosecutors didn't rely on this method (or any other?) since their witnesses babbled on with no guidance and kept saying things for the defense to attack on cross-examination.

They prosecutors should have pared down their list of witnesses to maximize their strengths, minimize their weaknesses and ultimately, win the case.

BIGGEST TRIAL MISTAKE #23:
The prosecutors failed to point out Trayvon's non-violent state of mind prior to the confrontation

The prosecutors failed to show Trayvon's calm and boyish state of mind while he was on the phone with Rachel Jeantel. He was worried about missing a game on television and told her to "go see if it started."

Also, he was concerned about the "creepy ass cracker" following him and balked at Rachel's suggestion that he might be a "molester."

"Don't even talk like that," Sybrina's child responded. And yet, the prosecutors never pointed out that Trayvon's reaction was meek, with no hint that he might retaliate or become violent to protect himself. It showed that his mindset was avoidance and that he had no intention to hurt his stalker. Rachel was his friend and peer. If he was aggressive, he would have bragged to her about what he would do if the stranger laid a hand on him.

But he didn't react like that. Instead, as GZ told the 911 operator, Trayvon ran away from him and out of sight behind the buildings.

BIGGEST TRIAL MISTAKE #24:
The prosecutors failed to argue that Trayvon had tried to avoid GZ

After they found GZ not guilty, one of the jurors said that Trayvon could have avoided being killed by simply going home. But that's what he was trying to do when he ducked behind a building and down a sidewalk to escape from the stranger who was following him in a car. He didn't know GZ had complained to 911, "These fucking assholes! They always get away!" and this time, the neighborhood watchman was determined not to let that happen.

And so, GZ got out of his car and chased Trayvon Martin until Rachel Jeantel heard him confront Trayvon with, "What are you doing around here?"

Ramona Rumph, the 911 operator, testified that GZ admitted he was following Trayvon and she told him, "We don't need you to do that." Regardless, GZ continued to follow the teenager. No matter what the juror said, it was clear to any reasonable person from the start of the chase that it was Trayvon Martin who had acted in self-defense to preserve his life, not GZ.

It was also possible that Trayvon was afraid to lead the "crazy ass cracker" to the condo where he was visiting his father because he didn't want to put his family in danger.

BIGGEST TRIAL MISTAKE #25:

Prosecutor Bernie de la Rionda failed to respect the seriousness of the occasion

A youngster was brutally killed without mercy. Regardless, Bernie De La Rionda, the lead prosecutor, cracked jokes, laughed, and made light banter with some of the witnesses. A few examples, he said, "Weren't you on the Olympic team but didn't get to go because of the boycott?" "Do you live alone in your apartment, except for your cat? What is your cat's name?" And, "When you stepped outside against your wife's advice, you made a fatal mistake, didn't you?"

The prosecutor wasn't funny at all and his attempts to be lighthearted were misplaced in a trial of the confessed killer who had shot a 17-year-old boy through the heart.

BIGGEST TRIAL MISTAKE #26:

The prosecutors failed to properly interpret what Rachel Jeantel said she heard Trayvon say

Rachel Jeantel testified she was having a conversation on her cell phone with Trayvon when GZ interrupted, saying, "What are you doing around here?"

Jeantel said that she heard Trayvon say, "Get off!" before she heard a thump and his cell phone went silent. It's reasonable to assume that GZ had shoved the boy and knocked the cell phone from his hand. However, the hapless prosecutors didn't understand this exchange and should have hired a linguist to translate it for the jury to make the point that GZ was the aggressor. Webster's defines aggression as being "an attack" or "hostile behavior." Therefore, it was clear that GZ was the aggressor in his confrontation with Trayvon.

Regardless, Don West made mincemeat of Rachel's story, and it would have been better if the prosecutors had not put her on the stand. Her testimony was not necessary to prove their prima facie case of second-degree murder. If the prosecutors had done their job right, they would have limited their witnesses to Trayvon's mother, the arresting officer, the medical examiner, and the firearms expert. They would have rested their case and forced GZ to testify.

BIGGEST TRIAL MISTAKE #27:

The prosecutors missed the clue that GZ had patted Trayvon down

It is reasonable to assume that the struggle between Trayvon and GZ started when the neighborhood watchman tried to pat the teenager down. Rachel Jeantel said that she heard, "Get off!" which meant "Take your hands off me!"

The volunteer neighborhood watchman was a wannabe cop. As such, when he put his hands on Trayvon, he was most likely intent on searching him for weapons. No doubt, Trayvon was offended and pushed him away.

Unfortunately, and negligently, the prosecutors didn't call an expert to explain what "Get off!" meant in the context of the confrontation. Not understanding African American English, they couldn't explain its true meaning to the jury.

BIGGEST TRIAL MISTAKE #28:

The prosecutors should have embraced the idea that GZ was a coward

By definition, wife beaters are cowards. They feel entitled to abuse their wives and will kill anybody who gets in their way. Or in GZ's case, they might even kill a complete stranger to intimidate a wife to keep her from leaving.

Even if this author is wrong that GZ's motive for killing Trayvon was to scare his wife into coming back to him, an alternative theory that the defense handed the prosecutors on a platter, but they failed to exploit, was that GZ was a coward. It was a better explanation for the killing than "because he wanted to," as John Guy had claimed in his opening statement.

Instead of embracing the defense's portrayal of GZ as a coward, the prosecutors tried to dispute it. That was a mistake, because they could have made it the theory of their case. Experts could have testified that most men can take a beating and get over it, but a coward can't ever let it go because he feels a deep humiliation and is driven to take revenge. That would have explained GZ's act of cowardice to save face during the struggle when he pulled his gun and shot Trayvon at close range.

BIGGEST TRIAL MISTAKE #29:
The prosecutors let the defense bully their witnesses

Too many times to list here, the prosecutors stayed in their seats and made no objections while their witnesses were being battered on cross-examination. Instead of asking questions like they were supposed to, the defense kept making speeches and scoring points with the jury. An example of this is when Syrdyka was on the stand.

> **O'Mara:** You assumed that GZ was the aggressor, but you don't have any evidence of that. You reached the conclusion based on finding out that the other person was a child. Based on your experience, there is a wide range of physical maturity, and a young boy could have a stronger voice from fairly high to deep, and it's based on your experience as a teacher.

The prosecutors should have jumped to their feet half a dozen times and yelled, "Objection! The defense is making speeches badgering the witness!" But they didn't move from their seats. Defeat was sapping their energy to fight back.

BIGGEST TRIAL MISTAKE #30:
The prosecutors failed to investigate how GZ really got his scrapes and bruises

The prosecutors failed to delve into the suspicious appearance of the good Samaritan right after GZ shot Trayvon. Jonathan Manola came out of his condo and took pictures of the shooter. Although photos of the victim sprawled in the grass could have brought him a big pay day for their sensationalism, Manola didn't take pictures of Trayvon. Inexplicably, when the prosecutors called Manola to testify, they never asked him to explain this odd behavior. Why not?

Manola could have been part of a conspiracy to kill Trayvon and cover up the crime. It's also possible that GZ's minor injuries were self-inflicted or that Manola could have hit GZ a few times to help him prove his claim of self-defense. Since this good Samaritan had discouraged his wife from getting involved when they heard the scuffle outside, a reasonable person would be suspicious and want to know why GZ's neighbor came out to take his pictures but didn't help his victim.

BIGGEST TRIAL MISTAKE #31:

The prosecutors failed to investigate a possible conspiracy or cover-up between GZ and Jonathan Manola

Following the gunshot, Syrdyka testified that she went to her window and saw a man stand up in the grass. He walked toward her and stopped at the condo next door. A light shone on his face from the porch and she saw GZ's profile. He put his hand up to his forehead like he was looking for someone through the neighbor's window. As if in response, Jonathan Manola came outside and approached the killer.

And yet, the prosecutors failed to follow up on this evidence of a possible conspiracy or cover-up of the killing. Unless he knew GZ was planning to kill someone, why would Manola venture outside after hearing a gunshot and face danger to himself from a man he didn't know? Or so he claimed in direct conflict to GZ who referred to him as "a guy I know".

Why didn't these prosecutors investigate the relationship and any prior contact Jonathan Manola might have had with GZ? Or whether they shared ideals about guns. There could have been an affinity or kinship around the Second Amendment right to bear arms. Or was it simply one white man helping another?

The prosecutors never even asked Manola or his wife why he took pictures of the scrapes and bruises on GZ's face and head but none of Trayvon. Very strange and suspicious.

BIGGEST TRIAL MISTAKE #32:

The prosecutors failed to test Trayvon's cell phone for blood and fingerprints

There was no testimony about where Trayvon's cell phone was found by the police. It was an important piece of the puzzle to pinpoint where the confrontation had really started. If the cell phone was left near the mailboxes, it would have confirmed where Rachel said Trayvon was when his phone went silent.

It is also possible that GZ had found Trayvon's phone and left blood or fingerprints on it. Or Manola, the good Samaritan, found it and that his prints and DNA were on it. However, we may never know because there was no mention about any forensic testing of Trayvon's cell phone. This is another failure that speaks volumes about the sloppy job done by these prosecutors.

BIGGEST TRIAL MISTAKE #33:
The prosecutors failed to keep in touch with the medical examiner and called him last instead of first

Dr. Shiping Bao, the medical examiner who performed the autopsy on Trayvon, was the last witness to testify for the prosecution. The prosecutors didn't keep in touch with him, and Dr. Bao was upset and got even with them. He "forgot" important details seemingly on purpose. Instead of allowing him to continue messing up their case, the prosecutors should have asked for a 10-minute recess to refresh his memory.

Once they got him alone, they should have apologized effusively and let him know how important he was to getting justice for Trayvon. Of course, they should have contacted him prior to that, but they may have assumed they didn't need to prepare a professional. Wrong!

A bumbling doctor giving a muddled report about how Trayvon died was not the last thing they needed the jury to hear before the prosecution rested its case. But he was.

From watching crime shows like *The Practice* and *Law and Order*, jurors are sophisticated and know how a jury trial should go. Starting with John Guy's opening statement from hell, these prosecutors didn't have a clue how a criminal trial was supposed to be conducted. They should have learned from the television prosecutors who only have an hour to make their case to call their most important witness first.

Instead, in an absurd waste of time and resources, these prosecutors took two weeks to call the medical examiner who performed the autopsy to prove the basic fact that GZ shot Trayvon through the heart. Instead of being the first, or even the second, Dr. Shiping Bao was their last witness.

Pissed off for being ignored for so long, the doctor "forgot" what was in his autopsy report and sandbagged their case with silly contradictions.

BIGGEST TRIAL MISTAKE #34:

The prosecutors blew Daniel Shoemaker's voir dire—he was the producer of the defense's animated re-enactment

In French, "voir" means "to see" and "dire" (sounds like "deer") means "to speak." Put together, "voir dire" is where a judge or lawyer questions a potential witness before they are allowed to testify at a trial.

Film maker Daniel Shoemaker produced a three-minute animation for the defense showing their version of the confrontation and final struggle between GZ and Trayvon. During Shoemaker's voir dire, O'Mara made numerous references to what GZ said had happened in the struggle, and the prosecutors said nothing.

Corey's team should have been on their feet, yelling "Objection!" Because the witness part of the trial was over and GZ didn't testify, Shoemaker's statements were hearsay and lacked the proper foundation.

While they wasted hours quibbling over the details of the animated reenactment, the prosecutors didn't see the forest for the trees and failed to raise the most obvious objection to stop the defense from showing the animation. The jury should never have seen it because GZ had chosen to remain silent. The film was a substitute for his testimony and a sneaky way to fill in the gaps of his side of the story.

BIGGEST TRIAL MISTAKE #35:

Prosecutors failed to pick up inconsistencies about where GZ said he had dropped the flashlight

In his video statement, GZ said that when Trayvon attacked him on the sidewalk, he dropped his flashlight. However, the police found the flashlight some distance away in the grass.

Unfortunately, the prosecutors used the killer's videos for evidence, putting themselves in the awkward (and stupid) position of trying to disprove most of it. Too bad they didn't review all the evidence beforehand and, perhaps, they wouldn't have made the foolish decision to use GZ's self-serving videos in their own case in chief.

It's possible that the flashlight was swinging in GZ's hand as he rushed toward Trayvon and he could have shone the light in the boy's face. Instinctively, the teenager would have swatted it away. Trying to defense himself from harm, Sybrina's child had the right to stand his ground and not be shot down.

BIGGEST TRIAL MISTAKE #36:
The prosecutors failed to use testimony that GZ was a coward, not a fighter

While GZ's witnesses testified that the neighborhood watchman was a coward because he didn't know how to fight, the prosecutors should have pointed out that's why he carried a gun! It was an equalizer and whenever he felt threatened, he was prepared to shoot to kill. Prowling around searching for intruders with a 9 mm Kel-Tec loaded with deadly hollow point bullets should have proved that Trayvon's killer had a depraved disregard for human life.

Although GZ was taught in his MMA class how to tap out, he chose to shoot a boy through the heart.

Following his acquittal, GZ's meanness and bullying proved to be true during his many confrontations with his estranged wife, who fled from their home. This was also evidenced when he blasted Jay-Z online and threatened to feed him to the Florida alligators. However, the former neighborhood watchman quickly shut his mouth after Snoop Dog checked him with a warning that his "bitch ass better not touch a hair on Jay-Z's head."

BIGGEST TRIAL MISTAKE #37:
The prosecutors underestimated the jury's sophistication

The human mind, especially when it's evil, is very complex. And more importantly, the jurors were trial savvy from television crime shows. No simple motive like "because he wanted to" could ever suffice to explain why the killer had shot an unarmed black teenager. The jurors wanted to know more.

In this age of 24-hour television, armchair sleuths demand that murder cases be wrapped up in a neat bundle with no strings left hanging. To satisfy them, the prosecutors needed to do more than discredit witnesses and expose their contradictory statements. The jurors felt cheated when the prosecutors never figured out why the volunteer watchman had done it and failed to give them the real motive.

Simple racial profiling didn't cut it while the jurors watched the black assistant rushing in and out to help the defense team. It didn't cut it after several black witnesses claimed there wasn't a prejudiced bone in GZ's body. Finally, it didn't cut it when John Guy and Bernie De La Rionda both assured them that he did it "because he wanted to." That was the lamest reason of all.

The prosecutors were so lost that they didn't even try to put the blame on the South and its racist history of setting white men free for killing blacks. Hello?

BIGGEST TRIAL MISTAKE #38:
The prosecutors were clueless that the Sanford police resented them and were not on their side

As stated elsewhere in this book, the prosecutors' biggest mistake was calling too many witnesses, most of which were hostile—especially from the Sanford law enforcement. After the attorney general snatched the case away from them and took over, the police officers were pissed. They were bitter about being replaced by outsiders, Angela Corey and her team.

Even though some of the officers thought GZ was guilty of manslaughter, there was no way Corey's team was ever going to get their full cooperation to convict him.

BIGGEST TRIAL MISTAKE #39:
The prosecutors failed to provide simple jury instructions

Some of the jury instructions needed to be simplified—especially since the prosecutors had to prove a double negative—that it was beyond a reasonable doubt that GZ didn't kill Trayvon in self-defense. Too confusing even for me, a career prosecutor.

Aside from the fact that the jurors didn't understand any of that legal mumbo jumbo in the instructions that appeared to be contradictory, the prosecutors failed to include an explanation of "manslaughter".

BIGGEST TRIAL MISTAKE #40:
The prosecutors failed to make the most of closing arguments

The prosecution always argues first, then it gets the last word after the defense puts on its case. By that time in closing arguments, Corey's team had to know they were in deep trouble. So why didn't they make the most of their last opportunity to explain in simple terms what their case was all about and which evidence had proved GZ guilty of second-degree murder or manslaughter?

Despite the prosecution's failure to include it in the affidavit of charges, the judge allowed an instruction about manslaughter without any help from the prosecution. Naturally, the jurors didn't understand it, and in the middle of deliberations they sent a note seeking clarification.

Unfortunately, Judge Nelson stonewalled them. In retaliation, the jury took it out on the prosecution and acquitted Trayvon Martin's killer.

BIGGEST TRIAL MISTAKE #41:
The good Samaritan's fists weren't checked for bruises or blood

It appears that the arresting officer or the other officers who arrived at the scene did not ask to see Jonathan Manola's fists to examine them for bruises or GZ's blood to determine whether the good Samaritan had inflicted the killer's injuries to his nose and on the back of his head.

BIGGEST TRIAL MISTAKE #42:
The prosecutors failed to heed warnings that they were losing

"We are confident that at the end of this trial you will know, in your head, in your heart, in your stomach, that George Zimmerman did not shoot Trayvon Martin because he had to. He shot him for the worst of all reasons: because he wanted to." That was how John Guy began his opening statement, and that explanation wasn't good enough for sophisticated jurors used to television detectives telling them in detail why a defendant committed a crime.

"Because he wanted to" left them hanging and didn't answer the question of "Why did he want to?"

The prosecutors made no effort to find the real motive behind GZ's decision to kill an innocent black teenager. As they continued to sink into the quicksand of their mistakes, the internet was blowing up with criticism. Pundits, lawyers, and the public warned Corey's team that they were mishandling the case. And while the jury was sequestered, the prosecutors were free to roam and hear what was being said. So why didn't they listen and take corrective action? At every stage of the trial they had opportunities to do things right and avoid making more mistakes. Why didn't they heed that advice?

BIGGEST TRIAL MISTAKE #43:
Prosecutors did not understand the elements of manslaughter and failed to explain them to the jury

The prosecutor's opening statement was from hell and the closing statement was boring as hell. In both they failed to excite the jury with a call for justice on behalf of Trayvon Martin and his grieving family. And worse, they didn't make it clear that the facts proved that GZ was guilty of manslaughter. GZ had recklessly killed Trayvon when he was not justified by self-defense.

Since the final confrontation took place in the grass, not on the sidewalk, GZ's head was not being bashed on the cement immediately before he pulled out his deadly weapon. Therefore, the killer's life was not in imminent danger and his claim of self-defense was bogus.

BIGGEST TRIAL MISTAKE #44:

The prosecutors failed to dispute GZ's lie that Trayvon had reached for his gun

In all three of GZ's video statements, he said his gun was in the holster behind his back. This conflicts with his claim that he had shot Trayvon when he reached for it. GZ said he was lying flat on his back. Therefore, unless the kid had x-ray vision, he could not have seen the pistol hidden under the neighborhood watchman's bulky jacket or even known it was there.

It made sense that when GZ whipped it out, it was Trayvon who started screaming for help.

BIGGEST TRIAL MISTAKE #45:

The prosecutors missed that GZ could have bashed Trayvon's head on the sidewalk

The confrontation started on the sidewalk. As they rolled around, GZ could have been on top and bashed Trayvon's head on the cement. Although his skull was somewhat protected by a hoodie and a thick afro, the prosecutors never even asked whether there was an examination of the teenager's head for injuries.

BIGGEST TRIAL MISTAKE #46:

The prosecutors failed to show Trayvon was not able to get a grip on GZ's slippery bald head

At the time of the struggle, GZ's head was shaved. You can't get a grip on a bald man's head, especially when it's raining. And it was pouring on the night of February 26, 2012 when the neighborhood watchman was supposedly on his back fighting for his life. And so, it was impossible for Trayvon to get a hold of his wet and slippery head to bash it on the sidewalk once, much else thirty times.

Unfortunately, by the time the trial began, GZ had a new image. He had grown a full head of hair and the prosecutors forgot that he used to be bald. As a result, they missed a crucial opportunity to punch a big hole in his story.

BIGGEST TRIAL MISTAKE #47:

*Prosecutors failed to explain why GZ, who was left-handed, had
strapped his gun on his right hip*

GZ was left-handed. But it seems that GZ had purposefully strapped
his gun on his right hip. So that he could surreptitiously reach behind his
back with his left hand to pull the weapon out?

Too bad the prosecutors didn't catch this possible evidence of
premeditation. They could have pointed it out to the jury to show the
killer's depraved heart and intent to commit cold-blooded murder.

BIGGEST TRIAL MISTAKE #48:

*Trayvon Martin deserved a more vigorous fight for justice than
Florida's lawyer's oath required of these prosecutors*

While most people blamed Florida's "Stand Your Ground" law or the
jury for not convicting GZ, the truth is that Trayvon Martin's family
deserved better prosecutors. Most states, like Ohio (where this author is a
prosecutor), require lawyers to take an oath promising to zealously and
diligently represent their clients. Unfortunately, Florida's oath lacks this
responsibility. It's a loophole that the GZ prosecutors slipped through to
escape accountability and discipline from the bar association for their poor
performance.

Regardless of Florida's low standards, these prosecutors should have
put forth their best efforts to fight for justice for Trayvon. Although it
came with the job when they took the GZ case, these prosecutors seemed
to feel no such obligation.

BIGGEST TRIAL MISTAKE #49:

The prosecutors failed to keep out the concrete block

Relevant and material evidence must relate to and be connected to the
facts and issues in the case. Perry Mason made "irrelevant and immaterial"
a familiar term for lawyers to object to evidence. Nowhere was this
objection more applicable than to the thick block of concrete that Judge
Nelson allowed the defense to use to prove that the sidewalk was a deadly
instrument.

The first objection should have been that the concrete block didn't come from any of the sidewalks at The Retreat at Twin Lakes, where the killing took place. Therefore, it was irrelevant and immaterial.

The second objection the prosecutors should have made was that admitting the block violated the rules of evidence for lack of a foundation. Every witness had testified that the final struggle took place in the grass, not on the sidewalk. Therefore, these prosecutors should have been screaming at the top of their lungs, "No foundation!"

The third objection the prosecutors should have made when the defense brought a block of concrete into court was that the cement block was dry. Therefore, it was not in the same condition as the wet sidewalk the night of the crime. It had been raining all evening, and the concrete on the sidewalk could have had puddles to cushion a person's head from injury should they slip and fall or otherwise find themselves prone on the sidewalk.

The fourth and most compelling objection the prosecutors should have made was that the injuries on GZ's head were minor scrapes. Therefore, there were no serious injuries that having his head bashed 30 times on a concrete sidewalk would have inflicted. The medical examiner testified that the volunteer neighborhood watchman had no smashed bones, no deep cuts, and no concussion.

BIGGEST TRIAL MISTAKE #50:
The prosecutors should have brought life-sized dummies to demonstrate the struggle

Trayvon Martin was a tall and skinny 140 pounds, while GZ was a stocky 200 pounds.

Regardless, the prosecutors brought in a 20-pound foam dummy instead of two dummies that were proportional to Trayvon's and GZ's body types. It would have been better if they had selected two random men of similar sizes from the spectators and had them wrestle in front of the jury.

That would have been more helpful than letting O'Mara sit astride the foam dummy and slap it around. In addition to having almost a century of trial experience among them, there were resources around the world the prosecutors could have called on to help design a more appropriate dummy to demonstrate the inconsistencies in GZ's video statements.

The old-fashioned dummy they presented in court for O'Mara to beat up should have had four arms to show the impossible feat that GZ accused Trayvon of: holding the grown man down with one hand, stifling his screams with a second hand, clutching GZ's bald head with a third hand, and bashing it thirty times on the sidewalk with a fourth hand.

BIGGEST TRIAL MISTAKE #51:
The prosecutors didn't have a black person on their team

GZ's lawyers were smarter than the prosecutors. Keenly aware that they had to combat the perception by the jury that GZ was a racist, black lawyers on their team kept scurrying in and out of the courtroom carrying files.

Certainly no blacks would be helping a racist go free.

The prosecutors needed blacks on their team just as much. Their victim was black. His family was black. A key witness, Rachel Jeantel, was also black. Even the 911 operator, Ramona Rumph, was black. So why did these prosecutors have the audacity to assume that they could deal with the dynamic between races that was at the center of their case without putting blacks on their team?

They also needed experts to help them interview and understand their witnesses of various races, help them select the jury, and help with every aspect of what happened that night when Trayvon Martin was shot and killed.

BIGGEST TRIAL MISTAKE #52:
The prosecutors failed to make timely objections

Before the trial started, the prosecutors should have reviewed the rules of evidence and criminal procedures because they didn't know when to apply them. "Objection! Asked and answered!" and "Objection! Beyond the scope of direct!" could have saved the prosecution's case or at least prevented the destruction of the testimony of their key witnesses.

For example, Syrdyka testified that she heard a shot while she was on a call with 911. Regardless, the prosecutors kept silent while O'Mara grilled her about the gun-shot she had already said she did not hear.

"You didn't see a muzzle blast?" "Fire out the end of a gun?"

"Did you ever see a flash out the barrel?"

"Can you reconcile that he was shot in the chest with what you saw?"

"Objection! Asked and answered!" Oops, that was this author, not the prosecutors.

BIGGEST TRIAL MISTAKE #53:

Prosecutors failed to have a forensics expert check the sidewalk for traces of blood

According to my sources, even after wear and tear and extensive washings, traces of blood can be found for days after a killing. The prosecutors did not even try to test the crime scene to prove that there was no blood and therefore, that GZ was lying when he said Trayvon banged his head on the sidewalk 30 times.

BIGGEST TRIAL MISTAKE #54:

Trayvon's hands were not examined for bruises or GZ's blood

My understanding of the medical examiner's testimony was that he didn't examine Trayvon's fists for bruises or blood. Also, the police officers didn't check GZ's hands or those of Jonathan Manola to see whether either of them was bruised or bloodied. It's possible that GZ's scratches and nosebleed were self-inflicted or caused by Manola or someone else after the shooting.

BIGGEST TRIAL MISTAKE #55:
The prosecutors waived "stand your ground" but should have known the jury would apply it anyway

Beware of the defense counsel bearing gifts. It was foolhardy for the prosecutors to agree to O'Mara's offer to waive the application of Florida's "Stand Your Ground" law to GZ's murder trial. The six ladies on the jury were very familiar with it anyway because they watched the Florida news, where people shot others and got away with it based on their right to use deadly force with no duty to retreat.

BIGGEST TRIAL MISTAKE #56:
Prosecutors failed to ask GZ's mother the right questions on cross-examination

John Guy was timid and treated GZ's mother with kid gloves. Apparently, the prosecutor did not want to offend the six mothers on the jury. However, he could have asked Mrs. Zimmerman whether her son told her what happened, including the fact that he had screamed before he shot Trayvon. If he had told her, then saying it was his scream was based on what he had told her. And if he had not told her, that would impeach and contradict her testimony that he had screamed.

These prosecutors behaved like they didn't know the basic rules of evidence. After Trayvon's mother recognized her son's scream during the Lauer 911 tape, they incorrectly assumed they had opened the door to the parade of defense witnesses, including the defendant's mother, who identified GZ's voice. That wasn't true at all.

Opinions expressed by a witness must be preceded by the proper foundation. This means that they had to show expertise or a basis for their opinion. However, every witness the defense called to identity the screams lacked expertise as voice analysts or lacked personal knowledge. They all admitted they had never heard GZ yell or scream before. Therefore, there was no foundation for their opinions, and the prosecutors should have been on their feet screaming, "Objection! Lack of foundation!"

Why these prosecutors continued to allow testimony that would ordinarily have been excluded adds to this author's suspicions that they were just going through the motions. They put on a show of prosecuting GZ when they were trying to lose.

BIGGEST TRIAL MISTAKE #57:
The prosecutors called 34 too many witnesses

Trotting out 34 unnecessary witnesses who were either hostile or not properly prepared to give relevant information to the jury about why Trayvon Martin was shot doomed the prosecution from the first day of the six-week trial.

BIGGEST TRIAL MISTAKE #58:
The prosecutors failed to uncover the whole truth before putting Jonathan Good on the stand

John Good's explanation of what was said between Trayvon and GZ when he stepped out of his condo did not make sense. Good testified that he saw two figures wrestling in the grass when someone said, "Help me subdue this guy."

It had to be GZ, because there was no way a black boy in Florida, the Deep South, would have asked a white man to help him subdue another white man. It makes more sense that when Good approached, Trayvon would have understood his predicament and said, "Help me! This dude jumped me for no reason. Please, call my dad!"

By the same token, it's more likely that GZ's true words would have been "Help me subdue this ni...r." Otherwise, if a white man had really said, "Help me subdue this guy," the normal reaction would have been to ask "Why? What did he do?" But Good claimed no other words were exchanged among the three of them. The person being subdued kept silent, and instead of asking what the fight was about or breaking it up, Good said he was going to call the police.

Then he turned on his heels and raced back to his condo. There should be little doubt in any reasonable person's mind that Good saw that the white man had the upper hand. Otherwise, I ask you, would he have left a white man on the ground at the mercy of a n----r?

Regardless of this logical analysis, the prosecutors called Good as a witness and never probed or questioned him any further to find out what had really been going on between GZ and his victim when he found them wrestling in the grass. As Alice observed about Wonderland, things kept getting curiouser and curiouser.

BIGGEST TRIAL MISTAKE #59:
The prosecution succumbed to the defense's use of the word "event" that desensitized the jury to a child's murder

Time after time, the prosecutors fell for O'Mara's scheme to desensitize the jury. It worked during the Rodney King trial when the defense replayed the video frame by frame and slowed down the beating to make it less horrifying. In this case, O'Mara kept referring to the killing of Trayvon Martin as an "event." The prosecutors sat on their hands while this took place hundreds of times, allowing the defense to reduce the seriousness of the offense from the taking of a boy's life to an event. Webster's defines an "event" as "an occurrence, especially of some importance." Of some importance? The killing of Sybrina and Tracy's teenaged son was of the utmost importance!

BIGGEST TRIAL MISTAKE #60:
The prosecutors didn't ask Jonathan Manola about GZ's second call to 911

GZ made a second 911 call that night that should have blown his claim of self-defense to smithereens. At 7:20 p.m., immediately after he had shot the teenager, the killer coolly contacted the emergency center again. Instead of calling for an ambulance, as he led Jonathan Manola to believe, GZ didn't say a word about shooting Travon. He merely repeated his earlier report of a suspicious guy hanging around.

This was a crucial piece of the puzzle that could have slammed the door on GZ's claim of self-defense. Had they pursued this line of questioning with Manola, they could have proved GZ's depraved disregard for human life. This cold-blooded man shot a boy through the heart and knew that every second counted for the paramedics to come save him.

However, GZ didn't want to save Trayvon's life for him to live and be able to tell what really happened.

Here is the official report of that second 911 call:

> Feb. 26, 2012 – 7:20 p.m.
> Type: TEL
> Subject: Suspicious activity
> Report: Repeats prior report

Now, compare it to the official report of GZ's first 911 call from only nine minutes earlier:

> Feb. 26, 2012 (night of Martin shooting) – 7:11 p.m.
> Type: TEL
> Subject: Suspicious activity
> Report: Black male "late teens dark gray hoodie jeans or sweatpants walking around area"…"subj now running towards back entrance of complex."

BIGGEST TRIAL MISTAKE #61:

The prosecutors never asked Jonathan Manola to take a lie detector test

The prosecutors were supposed to examine all the evidence and be skeptical when things didn't look right or make sense. Why did they accept the good Samaritan's unreasonable behavior without digging deeper? When they heard the commotion outside, Manola told his wife it was none of their business. He warned her to stay inside where it was safe. Then, suddenly, with no explanation, he went outside to take photos of a stranger who had just shot somebody.

To everyone except these prosecutors, Jonathan Manola's act of kindness toward GZ was highly suspicious. After he heard a gunshot, it made no sense for him (or anybody else) to leave the safety of his home to dash into the night into danger. Unless, of course, he knew there was no risk. And what happened next proved it when he took pictures of GZ's injuries and called his wife for him. The good Samaritan's story was so unbelievable that the prosecutors should have asked him to take a lie detector test before using him as a witness.

Why would Jonathan Manola take those pictures of GZ's injuries?

What was in it for him? What was so irresistible about putting his own life at risk? What had made him think he would not be harmed like the kid bleeding out in the grass?

It defied common sense that when a stranger shot somebody behind Manola's house his reaction was to rush outside to approach the guy. Why was Manola so interested in helping GZ if he didn't even know him? And why was he more interested in taking photos of GZ than the victim?

And since they didn't have the answers to these questions, why did the prosecutors call Manola as their witness? What he said didn't help their case at all.

BIGGEST TRIAL MISTAKE #62:
The good Samaritan's wife was not asked to take a lie detector test

Jeanne Manola, Prosecution Witness #11, said that she had stayed in the house after the gunshot. Her testimony added nothing to what had been said before, but it deepened the mystery of why her husband had gone out into the night to help GZ. The prosecutors did not even ask her how he explained leaving her to risk his life. These prosecutors had missed the obvious:

> that Mrs. Manola would have known about a conspiracy between her husband and GZ. They didn't bother her with questions to find out the real reason that Jonathan Manola went out to help GZ. And they did not bother to ask her what her husband told her when he came back home.

BIGGEST TRIAL MISTAKE #63:

The prosecutors never asked Jonathan Manola why he didn't call 911 when he saw Trayvon face down in the grass

Instead of calling 911 after he heard a gunshot like many other neighbors did, Jonathan Manola came out of his condo carrying his cell phone and took photos of GZ's injuries. Why didn't the prosecutors question this good Samaritan about his lack of concern for Trayvon's injuries and why he cared so much about GZ, a stranger?

BIGGEST TRIAL MISTAKE #64:

The prosecutors failed to catch GZ's whopping lie that he called 911 a second time to get help for Trayvon

Everyone has heard about GZ's first 911 call when he saw Trayvon in the neighborhood. Including the prosecutors, few people knew that GZ made a second call to 911 nine minutes later, after he had shot Trayvon. When he told Jonathan Manola about it, the good Samaritan assumed help was on the way for the victim. Of course, it wasn't, because GZ didn't mention to the 911 operator that he had shot Trayvon and he was watching him bleed out in the grass.

BIGGEST TRIAL MISTAKE #65:

The prosecutors failed to pick up on key evidence of a conspiracy

Prosecution Witness #18 Jayne Syrdyka said she was lying down in bed with her cat, Leo. She was reading with the television on mute when she heard a loud and dominant voice in the courtyard behind her condo. She opened the window to listen, but it was raining and dark out. One of the voices sounded aggressive and angry. A lighter voice with a softer pitch responded. She could not make out the words because the figures were 20 feet away. She turned the light off and saw the silhouettes of two people on the ground, one on top of the other. They were wrestling.

Then she heard what sounded like three popping noises. She saw a figure stand up and walk toward her window. That is when she saw clearly under the porch light that it was GZ. He put his hand up to shield his forehead like he was looking for someone through the window next door.

If the prosecutors had prepped her better, Syrdyka could have proven two crucial points for their case. One, that Trayvon had cried out for help, and two, that the struggle was in the grass and not on the sidewalk when the shot was fired. Instead, the prosecutors let Syrdyka ramble on during direct examination. And then, on cross-examination, she was manipulated by the defense and badly hurt the prosecutors' case by contradicting herself.

BIGGEST TRIAL MISTAKE #66:

The prosecutors had no idea what Syrdyka was going to say and not knowing hurt their case

Syrdyka testified that while she was calling 911, she heard three pops that she believed were gunshots. Unfortunately, it turned out there was only one shot fired. O'Mara had a field day with this contradiction and casted doubt on everything else Syrdyka said, including the crucial fact that the final struggle took place in the grass and not on the sidewalk.

Instead of guiding this witness to drive it home that the final struggle took place in the grass, the prosecutors let her babble on. This, of course, opened the door for the defense to ask dozens of questions on cross-examination that chipped away at her credibility. Her value as an eyewitness for the prosecution was destroyed.

BIGGEST TRIAL MISTAKE #67:

The prosecutors never asked Syrdyka to confirm that Trayvon was shot in the grass

State exhibits #41 and #44 were projected on the screen for the jury to see where Trayvon's body was when GZ got up and walked away. Missing the best chance they had during the trial to establish the exact spot where the struggle took place, the prosecutors failed to repair the damage by asking Syrdyka to confirm it. She could have testified emphatically that the final seconds of the confrontation did not happen on the sidewalk as GZ claimed because Trayvon's body was in the same place he was killed when the first police officer arrived.

BIGGEST TRIAL MISTAKE #68:
It was a losing strategy for the prosecutors to ask Syrdyka who was on top during the struggle

Like the Abbott and Costello routine "Who's on first?" the prosecutors got entangled in a foolhardy attempt to establish who was on top during Trayvon's fight for his life with GZ. It didn't matter! At any given moment during the struggle in the grass, either one could have been on top. The prosecutors wasted a lot of time trying to sort it out and confused the jurors when these positions were insignificant.

BIGGEST TRIAL MISTAKE #69:
Karyn Syrdyka's testimony was useless and damaged the prosecution's case

Whatever the prosecutors intended to gain from Syrdyka, this witness was not worth the damage she did to their case. The prosecutors watched helplessly while she struggled with her memory and rambled about her cat. It wasn't the jury's job to connect the dots between the holes in her testimony. Not one of them could ignore her inconsistencies.

Don West examined her account in painful detail and showed that she was not only forgetful but also biased. Syrdyka went on Anderson Cooper 360° to criticize the Sanford Police Department for conducting a lousy investigation. Jurors tend to believe that biased witnesses will lie.

These prosecutors failed to give instructions and keep tabs on their own witnesses. Of course, they didn't know about Syrdyka's posts on Facebook about the case.

BIGGEST TRIAL MISTAKE #70:
The prosecutors got kicked in the teeth for asking Syrdyka too many questions

Cross-examination is supposed to be confined to what the prosecutors asked the witness during direct examination. It's elementary that the questions on direct examination must be finely crafted to avoid opening up areas of weakness for the defense to probe into. Once again, the prosecutors did not have a plan or strategy to limit their questions. It was folly when they allowed Syrdyka to tell everything that happened that night. It was obvious that they had not spent any time with her to focus on the points they needed to score with the jury. And because they failed to keep in touch and meet with her, they opened up a minefield that blew up in their faces every time the defense posed a question.

Direct examination should have been limited to the fact that Syrdyka saw GZ in the grass as he got off Trayvon's body and went to meet Manola. That narrow focus would have stumped the defense and put questions in the jury's minds about a possible conspiracy with the man who had come out of his home to take pictures of the killer.

BIGGEST TRIAL MISTAKE #71:
The prosecutors failed to do a mock cross-examination with Syrdyka to check for inconsistencies

Syrdyka was Witness #11 for the prosecution. By then, their case should have been rock solid. However, if they really believed her testimony was essential to meet their burden of proof, which it wasn't, they should have gone over her testimony with her until she could keep her story straight without mistakes. Instead, Syrdyka was a hot mess of inconsistencies. For example, Syrdyka testified that that she had opened the window to hear what was going on outside. Then under cross-examination she contradicted herself and said that she had asked the 911 operator whether they wanted her to open her window. Although she tried to explain that she had closed the window before calling 911, Don West slammed her for being confused, and the jury could not ignore it.

BIGGEST TRIAL MISTAKE #72:
The prosecutors failed to rehabilitate Syrdyka

After the defense chops up their witness on cross-examination, the prosecutors have the right to ask follow-up questions to try to repair the damage done to their case. It's called "rehabilitation on redirect," and in this instance (one of hundreds), Corey's team didn't even try. The prosecutors could have rehabilitated Syrdyka by asking her whether she had opened her window and put it back down before she made the 911 call because it was raining. Instead, they let her contradiction lay like a concrete block of doubt in the minds of the jurors.

BIGGEST TRIAL MISTAKE #73:
The prosecutors failed to emphasize GZ's cold demeanor

Syrdyka was shaken and showed more emotion in her 911 call than GZ did from the moment he shot Trayvon. Although he had just taken the life of a child, he coolly peeked into a window to signal what appeared to be his accomplice, who came out and took pictures of his alleged injuries. (NOTE: This is the author's reasonable explanation for the good Samaritan's sudden appearance to photograph and offer help to GZ.)

BIGGEST TRIAL MISTAKE #74:
The prosecutors failed to bring their "A" game

People who watched the trial did not see much difference between the prosecutors and an episode of *The Three Stooges* where they pretended to be lawyers. They dropped papers, presented the wrong evidence to the judge, failed to ask the right questions to their witnesses, and did not object to the wrong questions being asked by the defense.

Could it be a coincidence that Angela Corey's team of seasoned litigators went blind, deaf, and dumb for the entire six weeks of GZ's trial? Hardly.

They had all practiced law in Florida and knew that they could not expect the jury to do the right thing. In order to get justice where black people are concerned, they knew they had to give the six women in the box no choice. So why didn't they present a tight case with a road map leading to GZ's conviction for second-degree murder?

BIGGEST TRIAL MISTAKE #75:
The prosecutors failed to understand the YouTube generation

There are 40,000 commercials on television every year. Not counting the programs, that's a lot of videos. And now advertisements pop up to try to sell us things while we are on our computers. We are used to being fed information with moving images and loud music. So how come the prosecutors didn't get it? They missed a great opportunity to tell Trayvon Martin's life story to the jury and take advantage of how powerful photos and videos could be.

Angela Corey's team could have asked Tyler Perry, Oprah, or Spike Lee to do a short to show how GZ had stalked and confronted Trayvon. It could have even been an open contest. This author, with a degree in film and television from NYU's Tisch, would have submitted a far better version than the stiff walking reenactment video from GZ's defense team. I would have cut and pasted the killer's voice over action that proved he was a pathological liar.

Unfortunately, there was no other visual to counter the defense's animation, and the animation was burned into the minds of the jurors.

BIGGEST TRIAL MISTAKE #76:
The prosecutors should have let Syrdyka tell the jury she didn't want to be a witness

When there is something negative about a witness, the jury wants to hear it from them. Otherwise, the witness appears to be deceptive and jurors will dislike them for hiding the truth. At first, Syrdyka was reluctant to get involved in the case. Who could blame her for not wanting to be the next target for her neighbor who was probably going to get away with murder? On cross- examination, the defense attacked Syrdyka about her efforts to remain anonymous.

> **Syrdyka:** "I was so shaken up; I didn't know what I was talking about." That shot her credibility, which the prosecutors could have avoided.

BIGGEST TRIAL MISTAKE #77:
Prosecutors sat quietly while the defense team attacked Syrdyka

> **Defense:** Didn't you go on television wearing a disguise
> to tell what you believe you saw and heard?
> **Syrdyka:** Yes.

Defense: You went on national television on the "Anderson Cooper" show to tell them that the Sanford Police Department failed to investigate the case enough, didn't you?
Syrdyka: Yes.

The prosecutors should never have called Syrdyka as their witness! She added nothing except confusion, and they did not need her to prove a single element of their case.

BIGGEST TRIAL MISTAKE #78:

The prosecutors asked Syrdyka an irrelevant question and failed to rehabilitate her on redirect

When they got the chance to question Syrdyka a second time following the cross-examination, the prosecutor asked only one question. The purpose should have been for her to answer the central issue about where the killing took place. She needed to be emphatic that she saw two people wrestling on the grass, not on the sidewalk, and that the gunshot immediately followed. Instead, the prosecutor asked whether or not the rain had obscured her vision when Syrdyka opened the window. Why would they want to impeach their own witness and make it seem that she hadn't seen anything at all? These prosecutors were off the hook!

BIGGEST TRIAL MISTAKE #79:

The prosecutors failed to have a firearms expert support Syrdyka's claim of hearing three pops

Syrdyka was ridiculed by the defense on cross-examination for hearing three pops following the single gunshot. It was possible that the sound ricocheted between the buildings. We will never know, because the prosecutors didn't call an expert to support what Syrdyka said.

BIGGEST TRIAL MISTAKE #80:

The prosecutors helped the defense prove that GZ reported prowlers in numerous calls to 911

Again, these prosecutors introduced evidence that helped the defense. This time, they asked Ramona Rumph, communications director for the Seminole County Sheriff, to tell the jury about the numerous calls that GZ had made before the night he shot Trayvon. The volunteer neighborhood watchman reported suspicious characters in his neighborhood on numerous occasions (See the Appendices), and these silly prosecutors helped the defense prove that he was just trying to protect his home and neighbors when he reported Trayvon.

BIGGEST TRIAL MISTAKE #81:

Time after time the prosecutors were forced to rebut GZ's three video statements that they had used for their own evidence

The prosecutors kept trying to contradict the evidence in GZ's video statements that they themselves had submitted into evidence! They broke a cardinal rule, never help the defense! Instead, they all but assured GZ's acquittal when they let the jury see and hear his story in his own words without being vetted by cross-examination. Like juggling with knives, the injuries suffered by these prosecutors were all self-inflicted.

BIGGEST TRIAL MISTAKE #82:

The prosecutors failed to put on crucial rebuttal witnesses

The prosecutors called a single witness on rebuttal and he didn't put a dent in GZ's story of self-defense. Incredibly, this witness was Adam Pollack, the gym owner who had testified for the defense that GZ was a failure in MMA training and was a coward.

BIGGEST TRIAL MISTAKE #83:

During closing arguments the prosecutors failed to dispute GZ's story that Trayvon bashed his head 30 times on the sidewalk

During closing arguments, the prosecutors failed to drive home the point that Jonathan Good, Prosecution Witness #17 for the prosecution, testified without later contradiction by anybody, that when he first stepped out of his first floor condo, he saw two people wrestling on the grass.

That meant that GZ had shot him on the grass and not the sidewalk!

BIGGEST TRIAL MISTAKE #84:

The prosecutors failed in closing arguments to underscore that GZ admitted he didn't move Trayvon's body that lay in the grass

Like the opening statement, the closing arguments by the prosecutors failed to underscore key evidence for the jury, including the fact that GZ consistently said that after he shot him, Trayvon fell over on the grass, and that's where he was found when the police arrived.

BIGGEST TRIAL MISTAKE #85:

The prosecutors failed in closing arguments to prove GZ's claim of self- defense was a fabrication

All the so-called eyewitnesses, along with the police, the forensics experts, and the three video statements from GZ proved that at the time he shot Trayvon Martin, they were on the grass and not losing consciousness from his head being bashed 30 times on the sidewalk. And so, the confessed was not put in fear of being killed and was not forced to kill the boy in self- defense.

BIGGEST TRIAL MISTAKE #86:

The prosecutors failed in closing arguments to show the jury conclusive forensics evidence that Trayvon was shot on the grass

Standing alone, the forensics evidence should have denied GZ's claim of self-defense because it would have proven beyond all doubt, reasonable or otherwise, that Trayvon was not bashing his head on the sidewalk at the moment he was shot through the heart.

BIGGEST TRIAL MISTAKE #87:

The prosecutors failed to keep the concrete block from being shown to the jury

The prosecutors failed to review the rules of evidence and criminal procedures that required the proper foundation before evidence can be admitted. The concrete block could not be authenticated because it was not an actual chunk from any sidewalk at The Retreat at Twin Lakes and so, it should have been excluded.

Furthermore, the concrete block lacked the proper foundation because Trayvon was not bashing GZ's head on the sidewalk at the time he was shot. Furthermore, the fact that GZ had no serious injuries to the back of his head, only scrapes, the block could not be used to substantiate those injuries.

BIGGEST TRIAL MISTAKE #88:

The prosecutors failed to prevent the defense from showing the concrete block to the jury because it was substantially different

The prosecutors failed to keep the defense's concrete block from being shown to the jury on the grounds that it was much thicker and not similar to any section of the actual sidewalk at The Retreat at Twin Lakes, and therefore, it was prejudicial and violated the Best Evidence Rule.

Under the Best Evidence Rule, the original is the best evidence whenever possible. Because the sidewalks at The Retreat at Twin Lakes were available, the defense was required to produce a section of it. When they didn't and brought a substitute, the prosecutors weren't familiar enough with the rule to make an objection.

BIGGEST TRIAL MISTAKE #89:

The prosecutors failed to investigate why GZ got rejected by the police academy

The prosecutors could have gotten somebody, either the other candidates or the teachers from the police academy, to give them information to tarnish GZ's do-gooder persona. It's amazing how people will hate on you if only you give them the opportunity.

The jury saw how law enforcement didn't stick together when the lead detective, Chris Serino, got on the stand and sabotaged the prosecutors. He was trying to send a message to the attorney general for going over the heads of the local authorities to name a special prosecutor.

BIGGEST TRIAL MISTAKE #90:

The prosecutors wasted time and money on an audio expert

The first time I heard the cries for help in the background of the Lauer 911 call, I was getting a snack in the kitchen, away from the television in my living room. The screams sounded like a child's voice, not those of a grown man. Judge Nelson disagreed that it was that simple. A month into the trial, she refused to allow the audio experts hired by the prosecutors to state an opinion on whether it was Trayvon or GZ who was screaming.

When Sybrina Fulton got on the stand and identified her son's voice, the door was opened for the defense, who contradicted her with a half dozen witnesses, including GZ's mother, who all swore that it was the defendant.

Who was screaming turned into another red herring that the prosecutors wasted time on instead of focusing on the evidence they already had to convict GZ of second-degree murder.

BIGGEST TRIAL MISTAKE #91:

The prosecutors slept while the defense lulled the jury to sleep with Amy Siewert's cross-examination

When the prosecutors called Florida Department of Law Enforcement firearms expert Amy Siewert, they didn't know how to use what she knew to advance their story. But O'Mara did. He took the excitement out of the gun talk by going into minute details to bore the jury. Instead of hovering on the edge of their seats, the jurors were anxious for the firearms expert to get off the stand. More points were scored for the defense.

BIGGEST TRIAL MISTAKE #92:
The prosecutors failed to convey to the jury the significance of how Trayvon was shot

Firearms expert Amy Siewert testified that the barrel of the gun was touching Trayvon Martin's hoodie when it was fired. It was a "contact shot" that proved GZ was up close and personal. The significance that the prosecutors failed to recognize and point out to the jury was that it was a deadly sucker punch. Because the killer and his victim were entangled, Trayvon didn't see it coming. He had no chance to defend himself. That's why he started screaming for help. Add the hollow point bullet that maximized the internal injuries, and GZ's depraved disregard for human life was evident. Unfortunately, this analysis went over the prosecutors' heads.

BIGGEST TRIAL MISTAKE #93:
The prosecutors failed to underscore the point that GZ's gun was fully loaded, plus he had put the fatal hollow point bullet in the chamber

Actions speak louder than words. This saying applies to GZ's motive for loading his gun with deadly hollow point bullets and why he put an extra bullet in the chamber of his pistol. What did it tell any reasonable person about GZ's state of mind when he strapped the holster to his body that night and went on the prowl for an intruder? The prosecutors should have emphasized for the jury that these premeditated acts showed a depraved indifference to human life.

BIGGEST TRIAL MISTAKE #94:

The prosecutors let the defense hammer away at the firearms expert without making objections

As usual, the prosecutors failed to properly prepare the firearms witness. As a result, Amy Siewert bent over backwards trying to be objective. However, if she were not going to express an expert opinion that was favorable to the prosecution, they never should have called her as their witness! Siewert blew many opportunities to blurt out her disgust about the gunning down of a child and let the jury know they should convict GZ.

An example of her failure to be proactive is when O'Mara asked, "Would you agree that all law enforcement carry their weapons ready to fire and they are of not much use unless they are ready to fire?"

Siewert replied, "Correct." She should have answered, "GZ is not a law enforcement officer, and cops never put an extra bullet in the chamber to kill children!" Of course, O'Mara would have objected and moved to strike her outburst. But it would have been too late. The jury would have heard it.

BIGGEST TRIAL MISTAKE #95:

The prosecutors should have studied the OJ trial and could have avoided the same mistakes

The GZ prosecutors showed arrogance and ignorance when they shouldn't have taken any chance on losing this high-profile case. Remember how fast the OJ prosecutors, Marcia Clark and Chris Whatshisname, sank into oblivion following their defeat in that open and shut case? Meanwhile, Johnnie Cochran and his dream team basked in the glory of victory and raked in millions of dollars.

Why didn't the GZ prosecutors study the videos of that trial? They could have learned a lot about how to avoid the same mistakes. Instead, they repeated most of the mistakes and invented new ones. For example, when these prosecutors brought a life-sized dummy into the courtroom, it was a repeat of the stunt that blew up in the faces of the OJ prosecutors when they made the wife-beater try on the gloves. That's when Johnny Cochran coined the winning phrase, "If it doesn't fit, you must acquit."

Although there was no catch phrase uttered when O'Mara sat on the prosecution's dummy and beat it up, that picture was worth a thousand words to the jury. I'll bet the GZ prosecutors still roll over in the middle of the night asking themselves why they took that chance.

BIGGEST TRIAL MISTAKE #96:

The prosecutors didn't know when to yell "Objection!"

These prosecutors should have taken refresher courses to learn how and when to make an objection. They botched it every time. For example, when O'Mara asked, "Would you agree that all law enforcement carry their weapons ready to fire and they are of not much use unless they are ready to fire?" De La Rionda should have yelled, "Objection! Beyond the scope of direct examination!" or "Objection! Beyond the scope of this witness's expertise. She's an expert in firearms, not their use by law enforcement!"

BIGGEST TRIAL MISTAKE #97:

The prosecutors never ordered GZ's flashlight tested for blood

Jonathan Manola could have bashed GZ's nose and head with the flashlight to make it look like self-defense. Or GZ could have hit himself with it. Either way, the prosecutors never tested GZ's flashlight for blood. For that matter, they didn't test Manola's cell phone either, which he had used to call GZ's wife.

BIGGEST TRIAL MISTAKE #98:

The prosecutors failed to prepare their firearms expert to score points with the jury

Whose witness was Amy Siewert, anyway? This firearms expert could have and should have turned the jurors against O'Mara for being cold and insensitive. Instead, Siewert helped the jurors fall into apathy about the killing of a high school student.

O'Mara asked, "From your experience in how it was utilized in this event, did it shoot its projectile the way it's supposed to?"

Siewert answered, "The gun functioned-yes—" However, if she had been properly prepared and in the right state of mind to help the prosecution, her reply would have been something like, "Yes, because it was fired at close range with a hollow point bullet that blew a big-ass hole through a 17-year old's chest like it was supposed to do!"

BIGGEST TRIAL MISTAKE #99:
The prosecutors failed to use the objection "Asked and answered!"
to stop the defense from bashing the firearms expert

Jurors are only human, and as such, their minds are prone to wander when sitting for long periods of time. Repetition is the tactic that clever lawyers like O'Mara employ to drive home a crucial point to the jury, who might have slept through it earlier. However, it's the prosecutor's job to yell "Objection! Asked and answered!" to prevent the defense from repeating testimony to help win their case. For example, O'Mara asked, "Did it shoot its projectile the way it's supposed to?"

Siewert answered: "The gun functioned, yes."

O'Mara then asked, "And it worked the way it was supposed to?" The prosecutor missed their cue and should have jumped up with, "Objection! Asked and answered!" Instead, they let Siewert repeat her answer. Were the prosecutors nodding off, or did they just not give a damn?

BIGGEST TRIAL MISTAKE #100:
The prosecution failed at rebuttal

While they let the defense put on witnesses who attested to GZ's good character, the prosecutors failed to counter with rebuttal witnesses to prove he was a liar and a deceiver. Instead, Corey's team was out of gas and rolled over like a dog playing dead.

BIGGEST TRIAL MISTAKE #101:

The prosecutors failed to rebut the defense's closing argument that if the jury used common sense, they would find GZ not guilty

It appeared that common sense went out the window. On rebuttal, the prosecutors should have argued that if the jurors applied common sense to the facts, they would convict GZ. He loaded a gun with deadly hollow point bullets, got into his car, and chased down an unarmed teenager. Although he had called 911 and been advised not to follow the child, GZ jumped out of his car and confronted him. During the struggle in the grass, the neighborhood watchman pulled his weapon, pressed it against the boy's chest, and fired. There was no exit wound because the hollow point bullet imploded inside Trayvon's chest and tore his heart apart. The killer got up, re-holstered his weapon, and went to the window of the condos. A so-called good Samaritan came out and took pictures of the scrapes and bruises on his nose and scalp. A flurry of 911 calls summoned the police, and when an officer arrived, GZ confessed to shooting the lifeless boy in the grass and surrendered his weapon.

The prosecution has the right to speak first and last to the jury during closing arguments. For reasons known only to them, the GZ prosecutors failed to take advantage of the opportunity to make the last impression on the six women in the box. Instead of arguing that the above scenario required them to find GZ guilty of second-degree murder or manslaughter, Corey's team called a single rebuttal witness. He was defense witness Adam Pollock, the instructor at the gym who said GZ failed to learn how to fight because he was a coward.

Why on earth would the prosecutors let the last person the jury heard confirm the defense's irrational argument that Trayvon was the aggressor because GZ was too chicken to fight back when his life was at stake?

BIGGEST TRIAL MISTAKE #102:

The prosecutors failed to argue that GZ had killed Trayvon in cold blood

Even if Trayvon had managed to get on top of GZ, he didn't do much damage to the neighborhood watchman, because all he had was a bruised nose and a few scrapes on the back of his head. How he got those injuries was very suspicious. Knowing he was on the hook for murder, GZ could have smashed himself with his flashlight, or the good Samaritan who came out to offer help could have done it for him. Either way, having only a few scrapes and bruises proved he was not beaten to the point where he had to kill to save himself.

Boys will be boys. You give a whupping and you take a whupping. However, in GZ's mind, this was no ordinary fight. The prosecutors got it right that he shot Trayvon through the heart because he wanted to. But why he wanted to was the biggest hole in their case. Although the evidence of GZ's depraved indifference to human life was there for all to see, the prosecutors failed to put the pieces of the puzzle together to convince the jury that GZ was guilty of second-degree murder.

Trayvon was unarmed. And he didn't know that GZ had an automatic pistol loaded with deadly bullets concealed in a holster on his back. In their ramblings about the case in closing arguments, the type of bullet was the key point the prosecutors failed to make to prove the killer's depraved indifference to human life. Because it would implode on impact and destroy tissue and bones, it was the bullet of choice for combat to stop the enemy.

This act was premeditated: GZ loaded his gun with hollow point bullets before he went out to patrol his neighborhood, and when he fired into the child's chest, the killer knew he was never going to get up.

BIGGEST TRIAL MISTAKE #103:
The prosecutors failed to argue that GZ was immature

Any mother can tell you how fast an eight-year old can make up a lie to get out of trouble. And while these lies make perfect sense to the adolescent, an adult can see right through them. But not these prosecutors. GZ's immature fabrications went over their heads.

He quoted Trayvon as saying, "You got me!" But GZ probably said "I got you!" and switched it up. His kindergarten story that he was walking down a path when a kid jumped out of the bushes and declared, "You're going to die tonight!" would be laughable except that an armed man shot a child through the heart when all he did was go out to buy an Arizona Iced Tea and a bag of Skittles.

Immaturity was the major factor that led to the killing and was the key to understanding everything GZ did. He had an adolescent fascination with becoming a police officer. And when he failed, he did the next best thing.

He bought a gun and joined a group of neighborhood watchmen to patrol for intruders. Of course, he was the most extreme and pestered 911 with calls. GZ fancied himself to be their leader and the savior of the community.

But his wife, Shellie, knew he was far from a saint. His cool demeanor was fake. He bullied her, was delusional, and acted self-centered. He was a loose cannon and she was scared for her life. Marrying him was a huge mistake, and the night before GZ killed a black kid, she fled to the safety of her father's home. And when GZ got out on bail, he badgered her into coming back. It was very possible that he had threatened to kill her if she didn't stand by him.

BIGGEST TRIAL MISTAKE #104:

The prosecutors failed to order a mental exam of GZ

A sociopath has no conscience and a pathological liar lies at the drop of a hat. GZ showed symptoms of both personality disorders from the moment he called 911 and was told to stop following Trayvon to when he told Sean Hannity "it was God's plan" for him to kill Trayvon. Despite it all, the prosecutors treated the cold-blooded killer like he was normal, just mean, and ignored his craziness. At least if the tests had revealed that he had a mental illness and he pleaded to insanity, the mad man would have been committed to an institution and pulled off the streets.

BIGGEST TRIAL MISTAKE #105:

The prosecutors should have argued that Trayvon would have respected a white man until GZ put his hands on him

It appeared to be knee-jerk racism when GZ selected Trayvon because being black made him an easy target. However, the teenager's first reaction would have been to respect a white man. In the dark, the teenager couldn't tell that GZ was mixed and his mother was Peruvian.

This was Florida, the Deep South, and Trayvon knew the rules. That's why he tried to get away in the first place to avoid trouble.

But when GZ hunted him down and put his hands on the black teenager, the rules changed. Trayvon went into defensive mode and stood his ground like he had the right to do under Florida law. "Get off!" he declared in self-defense. That's exactly how anybody would have reacted to a stranger touching them. And if he persisted, which apparently GZ did because he was a bully with murder on his mind, the fight was on. You don't load your 9 mm with deadly hollow point bullets and put an extra one in the chamber unless you are planning to kill somebody.

BIGGEST TRIAL MISTAKE #106:
The prosecutors opened up Syrdyka's history as a teacher and the defense pummeled her for being a lousy voice expert

Once again, Syrdyka fell into a trap set by the clever defense team. Unlike the prosecutors, O'Mara and West had brushed up on their skills before going into battle.

> **Defense:** "You never heard his voice before?"
> **Syrdyka:** "I heard it that night when I opened the window."
> **Defense:** "But you had never heard GZ'S voice before?"
> **Prosecutor:** "OBJECTION! Asked and answered!"

Just kidding, that's what I wished they had said but the prosecutors sat on their brains and allowed Syrdyka to answer.

> **Syrdyka:** "No."

The defense's trap was sprung. Sydyrka had testified on direct examination that earlier she had heard two voices arguing, one meek and the other strong.

BIGGEST TRIAL MISTAKE #107:

The prosecutors failed to capture the jury's imagination

The prosecutors were not familiar with the term "KISS," which stands for "Keep It Simple, Stupid." All they had to do was prove that Trayvon was shot through the heart and died almost instantly and that GZ had confessed to a police officer at the scene. The burden would have shifted to the defense team to prove that he had acted in self-defense.

Since there were no witnesses to the killing, GZ would have been forced to get on the stand to convince the jury of his innocence. However, that would never have happened because the inconsistencies in his video statements made the killer a sitting duck for the prosecutors to attack and prove he was a liar.

As a result, O'Mara would have made a deal for the lesser charge of manslaughter. These prosecutors would have won by default. Instead, they called every witness they could think of in a mindless order.

BIGGEST TRIAL MISTAKE #108:

The prosecutors called a medical examiner who didn't perform the autopsy

"Irrelevant and immaterial" means not having anything to say that matters. Therefore, the entire testimony of Witness #27 Dr. Valerie Rao was irrelevant and immaterial. Although Dr. Rao was a state medical examiner, she was not the one who had performed Trayvon's autopsy. As a result, she had no involvement in the case and was just another unnecessary witness in the prosecutors' dog and pony show. Furthermore, the jury did not need this so-called expert to tell them what they could see for themselves: that in the photos of GZ's face and head, his injuries were "minor" and "very insignificant."

BIGGEST TRIAL MISTAKE #109:

The prosecutors failed to make the right closing arguments

Another colossal mistake the prosecutors made was not making a PowerPoint presentation of GZ's lies and inconsistent statements during closing arguments. For example, Jonathan Good, who had stepped outside during the struggle, said he didn't know GZ. However, the killer referred to him as "a fellow I know." The prosecutors didn't catch this discrepancy or many other contradictions in the testimony of the witnesses, who should have been investigated for a conspiracy or a cover-up.

BIGGEST TRIAL MISTAKE #110:
The prosecutors failed to wrap the case up in a neat package

If the prosecutors had done their job right, the jury would have convicted GZ of manslaughter or second-degree murder. However, Corey's team didn't know the motive for the killing, so they started out losing. It was downhill all the way, and when the trial was done, they left too much for the jury to sort out. It didn't help that Judge Nelson refused to clarify their question about the elements of manslaughter. Whose side was she on? It certainly didn't appear to be justice..

ONE BIG MISTAKE MADE BY THE DEFENSE:
THEY DIDN'T GET PAID!

After GZ's acquittal, a reporter asked Mark O'Mara what advice he wanted to give GZ about the future. O'Mara barked, "Tell him to pay me!" Once a scoundrel, always a scoundrel. The entire defense team, if they ever believed in GZ's innocence, had to have serious doubts and learn a lesson from the movie *Anatomy of a Murder*.

The murder suspect in *Anatomy of a Murder* was acquitted. He hastily blew town, leaving his lawyer a note that said he had the irresistible impulse to get the hell out of town without paying his legal bill. Like that killer's lawyer, Lead Attorney Mark O'Mara didn't turn out to be a good judge of character. Despite his victory in getting GZ acquitted, the last laugh was on him. GZ stiffed him for two million dollars in legal fees!

<h1 style="text-align:center">10</h1>

<h1 style="text-align:center">HOW THEY COULD HAVE WON</h1>

Convicting a killer who had confessed at the scene should have been easy. However, the GZ prosecutors blew this high-profile case from the start. For reasons understood only by them, they failed to apply the rule of KISS (Keep It Simple, Stupid). Instead of streamlining their presentation, they trotted out every witness they could find (38 in all!) and threw other evidence at the jury for them to sort out for themselves. Overwhelmed and resentful, the jurors took the easy way out and found GZ not guilty.

And now, 7 years later, Angela Corey's team still denies responsibility for the countless mistakes in judgment that they made and blew the only chance that anybody would ever have to hold GZ criminally responsible for killing Trayvon Martin, an unarmed 17-year old.

<h2 style="text-align:center">FIRST:
THEY NEEDED ONLY 4 WITNESSES</h2>

At the scene of the killing, GZ confessed and made the prosecutors' job simple. To make him get on the stand where they could tear his lies and inconsistencies apart on cross-examination, all they needed were four witnesses. To prove a prima facie case of second-degree murder they should have called four people.

First, the officer who took GZ's confession; second, Trayvon's mother to confirm that her son was the victim; third, the medical examiner who did the autopsy to explain how Trayvon was killed; and fourth, the firearms expert to explain how the bullet that GZ fired exploded on impact and blasted a hole so big in Trayvon's chest that recovery was impossible, showing a depraved indifference to human life.

Instead of limiting their case to these four witnesses, the prosecutors called 34 unnecessary witnesses, and in the worst strategy of all, they showed GZ's three video statements to the jury. GZ's defense counselors sighed in relief that he was let off the hook and spared a long prison term.

Prosecution Witness #34 was Amy Siewert, the firearms expert whose testimony was crucial to prove that GZ had fired a hollow point bullet that imploded on impact in Trayvon's chest. If she had been properly questioned by the prosecutors, Siewert could have established that the purpose of hollow point bullets is to do unrecoverable damage to the victim. This would have shown a depraved indifference to human life, a main element of second-degree murder.

SECOND:
THEY SHOULD HAVE FORCED GZ TO TESTIFY

Self-defense is an affirmative defense, which means the defendant has the burden to prove it beyond a reasonable doubt. Therefore, the singular goal of the prosecutors should have been to force GZ to get on the stand and tell his story. On cross-examination, they could have used the killer's inconsistent statements to trap him.

Instead of taking this short path to victory, the prosecutors projected GZ's three video statements filled with inconsistencies on a screen for the jury to watch. If the Defense had tried to submit them into evidence, the court would have excluded them under the Hearsay Rule. "Hearsay" is a statement made outside the court and is excluded because it was not subjected to cross-examination to determine whether it was true.

In a move previously unheard of during any criminal trial, Angela Corey's team gave the defense a gift and allowed Trayvon's killer to sit back and avoid the pressure of cross-examination. As a result, the prosecutors blew the only chance anyone would ever have to hold the volunteer neighborhood watchman accountable for taking the life of Sybrina Fulton and Tracy Martin's unarmed child.

Instead of praying for the right outcome, as Bernie De La Rionda claimed he had done, the trial should have been based on specific facts and a foolproof strategy to prove beyond a reasonable doubt that GZ was guilty of second-degree murder.

THIRD:
THEY SHOULD HAVE FOLLOWED
12 RULES FOR WINNING A JURY TRIAL

What else did Angela Corey's team, who were supposed to know their way around a Florida court room, do wrong during the six-week trial? They failed to follow the following twelve rules for winning a jury trial:

WINNING RULE #1:
Develop the theory of your case, including the motive

Based on the evidence you gather, the theory of your case is the story you tell the jury to answer how, when, where, and why the defendant committed the crime.

Each one of these elements is important. Forget or leave one unexplained and you lose the trial, like the GZ prosecutors did when they failed to provide a believable motive to explain why the neighborhood watchman had shot the unarmed 17-year-old. "Because he wanted to" from John Guy's opening statement just didn't cut it. Today's juries are savvy from crime shows. To satisfy them, Angela Corey's team should have conducted a more thorough investigation into the killer's family, his friends, and his associates to find out GZ's real motive.

In this author's opinion, the neighborhood watchman killed Trayvon Martin in what appeared to be an act of domestic terrorism. GZ had abused his wife who had left him the previous night. As a result, it was reasonable to assume that he took an innocent boy's life to put his wife in fear that he would kill her too if she didn't come back to him. And it worked. Although she was scared out of her wits, Shellie made a beeline back to GZ and sat stoically behind her husband throughout the trial.

Despite all the headlines and statistics about killings in abusive relationships when a wife tries to leave, the prosecutors missed this big clue that would have explained how GZ became unhinged and violent. Although this case followed the typical and tragic scenario, Corey's team floundered and were unable to figure out why GZ had killed an unarmed boy who had simply gone out to buy a bag of Skittles. Predictably, as soon as the trial was over, Shellie fled once more to her father's home and filed for divorce.

WINNING RULE #2:

Prepare your witnesses and keep them close

From start to finish, it was apparent that the GZ prosecutors had little contact with their witnesses. From the disjointed manner in which most of them testified, none of them were prepped either for direct examination or for the brutal cross-examination by O'Mara and West. The prosecutors should have kept in touch with their witnesses and even coddled them until the day they walked into the courtroom.

Although it's unethical to rehearse what they will say, no prosecutor should ever call a witness when they haven't reviewed at least several times what they know and how it fits into the theory of their case. Also, savvy government prosecutors who have the resources and really want to win hold mock cross-examinations to evaluate how their witnesses hold up under pressure.

If a prosecutor determines that a witness can hurt their case, they have time to figure out a way to prove the same thing without them. In too many instances the GZ prosecutors used witnesses that contributed nothing to their case and were more helpful to the defense.

WINNING RULE #3:

Reach out to the community for help

Evaluate your evidence with a keen eye then reach out for help to organizations and the legal community if you perceive weaknesses in your evidence. The vast resources of universities and organizations are available to lend their expertise to important causes. Unfortunately, the GZ prosecutors were too arrogant or stubborn to seek the outside assistance that they sorely needed.

WINNING RULE #4:

Know the judge and the defense team

Before going into battle, a prosecutor must research and know everything about the judge and the defense team, including their usual tricks. It is helpful to contact lawyers who practiced in the criminal division to find out about your opponents and how the judge assigned to your case handles motions and rules on evidence.

Never go into court unless you know what you are up against.

WINNING RULE #5:

Practice your case before a focus group

Find out whether you have a winner or a stinker. Perform your opening and closing arguments in front of a focus group for an impersonal evaluation of you and your case. Then polish your presentation based on their comments.

WINNING RULE #6:

Hire a jury selection expert

Some lawyers take more time picking their ties than they do picking the people who will determine whether the defendant goes home or goes to jail. Don't gamble with your outcome. Hire a jury selection expert to profile the ideal jury according to who the defendant is and the crime you must prove that he committed.

WINNING RULE #7:

Force the defendant to testify or plead out

Self-defense is an affirmative defense, which means that after the prosecution rests its case, the defense has the burden of proving it beyond a reasonable doubt. Except, of course, when the prosecutors prove it for them like the GZ prosecutors did when they used GZ's video statements as part of their own case.

If they had not done that, the neighborhood watchman would have been forced to plead out or get on the stand to explain why he was in fear of his life and had to kill an unarmed boy. Under cross-examination, the prosecutors could have trapped him in any lies and inconsistencies. Instead, the jury got to see and hear the killer's unchallenged version of the shooting.

WINNING RULE #8:
Charm and never curse at the jury

Studies show that most jurors make up their minds during the opening statement based on which lawyer they liked best. And so, you must shine and put on your best manners. If they like you, they will believe what you tell them.

Impress them with your knowledge of the facts and never read from your notes. Avoid big legal words and tell your story in plain talk with no profanity. Prosecutor John Guy didn't get the memo before making his opening statement. He started off on the wrong foot with "Fucking assholes! They always get away!" Although it was a direct quote from GZ's 911 call, it was offensive to the six women in the jury box.

It was sheer luck that the abrasive and non-smiling Don West made it a dead heat when he blew the defense's opening statement with a knock-knock joke. "Knock-knock. Who's there? George Zimmerman. George Zimmerman who? All right, good, you're on the jury."

West's joke landed with a thud. Six stony faces stared at him from the jury box.

"Nothing? That's funny," he said, trying to get them to laugh. Still, the women in the box remained silent while Lead Defense Counsel Mark O'Mara stood with his mouth open, stunned by his partner's stupid attempt at humor.

Unfortunately, the prosecutors didn't take advantage of the opportunity that West gave them to regain lost favor with the jury, and their case slid further downhill.

WINNING RULE #9:

Bring your victim back to life in the courtroom

Your victim and the story of his life is the heart of your case. Bring him back to life in the courtroom through photos, videos, and stories from his loved ones, especially his mother, that will bring the jurors to tears. Reveal the qualities that show he was a loving child, brother, and human who laughed and enjoyed life. Share his goals, achievements, and dreams that will never be fulfilled because of the defendant.

The most glaring omission from GZ's trial was Trayvon Martin's story. I never knew him, and thanks to the prosecutors who failed to bring him back to life in the courtroom, I didn't learn much about him either.

Perhaps, they were afraid to put his life on display because he had smoked pot and been in trouble at school for writing graffiti on the walls. So what? They should have included these minor breaches of the rules as normal stuff that kids do. They made Trayvon human and more sympathetic to the jury. And his demise was more tragic since the chance for him to rise above this phase and redeem himself in the future was taken away by his killer.

WINNING RULE #10:

Make the defendant the villain of your story

While you glorify the victim, villainize the defendant. Never show him respect or refer to him by name like the prosecutors did throughout the trial when they kept calling Trayvon's killer "Mr. Zimmerman." They should have referred to him only as "the defendant," the "man who took the victim's future," "that "heartless thing at the defense table," or even "Trayvon's confessed killer."

You won't get away with calling him a monster except during opening and closing statements. However, you and your witnesses can try, especially during outbursts of grief from the victim's mother. The defense will object strenuously and the judge will scold you, but the jury will have heard it. Remember, you can't un-ring the bell.

WINNING RULE #11:
Never help the defense

It's elementary that you should never provide any evidence or witness that helps the defense prove its case. But somehow, this axiom flew over the heads of the GZ prosecutors. Time after time, they foolishly introduced documents and testimony that helped the defense while destroying their own case. A prime example was the use of GZ's video statements, in which the killer gave conflicting versions of what had happened that fateful night in Sanford. Ordinarily, the defense would have been blocked from showing the videos to the jury because they contained hearsay and were self-serving. Instead, the prosecutors showed them in their entirety while Mark O'Mara and Don West exhaled in relief. It was a gift to them and meant that GZ didn't have to testify to prove his claim of self-defense.

Incredibly, these prosecutors projected GZ's 3 video statements on a screen for the jury to watch and hear his version of the story. Then Corey's team spent the rest of the trial trying to disprove and explain away everything they themselves had shown that the killer had said. How absurd!

In 1995, during OJ Simpson's trial, every prosecutor, including myself, had the rare opportunity to learn important tactics and trial procedures as they unfolded before our eyes for nine months on television. Nobody can forget Prosecutor Darden's colossal blunder when he made OJ put on those gloves. It became fodder for Johnny Cochran's winning slogan, "If they don't fit, you must acquit!"

Now here is a slogan for the GZ prosecutors: "If the Defendant doesn't take the stand, don't show the jury his video statements!" Okay, it doesn't rhyme and lacks Johnny's punch line. However, it says what Corey's team needed to hear. Unfortunately, it comes much too late to be of any use.

WINNING RULE #12:
Never ask a question you don't know the answer to

It's the cardinal rule you learned in law school: Never ask a witness a question you don't know the answer to because you can get burned by a terrible surprise that damages your case. Every question is akin to a spider weaving a web, with each answer entangling the witness deeper into your version of the facts. That's why a lawyer's best friend is a leading question that must be answered with "yes" or "no."

Open-ended questions start with "Why…?" and allow the witness to take you down a path where you don't want to go. Too many times the GZ prosecutors ventured into unknown territory, asking witnesses why and ending up with slime on their faces. An example of this is Prosecution Witness #15, Selma Mora, who lived at The Retreat at Twin Lakes. On June 27, 2013, the fourth day of the trial, she was called to the stand. Her English was poor, and she testified in Spanish and used an interpreter. Unfortunately, the prosecutors didn't have a clue what she was really saying. And the problem was that one juror was Latino and others might have understood the language and Mora's extraneous comments while they didn't.

Even worse, on cross-examination, Mark O'Mara asked Mora to come down from the stand to demonstrate how she went to her door. There wasn't a person watching the trial who needed to be shown how somebody walked. This misuse of a prosecution witness stunned Corey's team and they didn't know how to fix it. Of course, they should not have called Mora to testify in the first place. Like many witnesses who preceded and followed her, she was useless because she didn't see the struggle between Trayvon and GZ.

11

"NOT GUILTY!"

On Saturday night, July 13, 2013, following two days of deliberations, the six female jurors found George Zimmerman not guilty of second-degree murder. They set 17-year-old Trayvon Martin's confessed killer free despite the undisputed fact that he had shot the kid at close range with a semi- automatic pistol that he later sold for $250,000.

WHAT THE DEFENSE COUNSEL SAID:

While celebrating his victory, Lead Defense Counsel Mark O'Mara, said if it had been the other way around and Trayvon Martin had killed GZ, he never would have been charged.

That statement defies Florida's history. If the Sanford police had arrived to find that a white man, even a half-white man like GZ, was shot by a black kid with a loaded gun, he would have been shot down on sight. No one would have heard or cared about his claim of self-defense.

WHAT THE PROSECUTORS SAID:

One of the most baffling statements made by the GZ prosecutors after the not guilty verdict was that they didn't choose their witnesses. They claimed that they were stuck with the 38 they had called to testify. Nonsense! Like every prosecutor, it was their responsibility to sort out and pick the best witnesses. No one required them to put any particular person on the stand. It was their job to develop a theory of the case and to subpoena only the witnesses who could prove the elements of second-degree murder. And despite their failure to charge GZ with manslaughter, an easier crime to prove, they could have pulled it off. They only needed four witnesses (Trayvon's mother, the arresting officer, the medical examiner, and the firearms expert) to force GZ to testify and win their case during cross- examination.

Special Prosecutor Angela Corey continues to call GZ "a murderer." Of course, she knows very well that by statute "murderer" is a legal term that only applies to individuals convicted of the crime of murder. Somehow, she believes slinging the word around will impress people with her sincerity and absolve her from the responsibility of blowing an open and shut case.

The big mystery that still lingers is not whether GZ killed Trayvon in cold blood—the evidence was overwhelming that it was an execution—but why didn't the prosecutors give a damn? Was their mishandling of the case due to ignorance, apathy, or arrogance? Did cock-eyed prejudice keep them from seeing straight because they believe that black youth are all up to no good?

PEACEFUL PROTESTS AND DEMONSTRATIONS

On July 13, 2013, after the shocking verdict, law enforcement across the nation got prepared for riots and buildings to be burned down. They were wrong.

From coast to coast, outraged citizens poured into the streets for several days. However, they remained calm during peaceful demonstrations.

Children wiped tears from their faces during a youth service at the St. Paul Missionary Baptist Church in Sanford.

At the Seminole County Courthouse in Sanford, mothers sobbed and held their children close while others waved "Justice 4 Trayvon" and "Jail the Killer!" One lone demonstrator dared to carry a sign, "We love you, George!" The protestors remained calm despite efforts to provoke them into violence. But there was simmering bitterness in historically black Goldsboro, where a man wore a t-shirt with George Zimmerman's likeness in the cross-hairs of a rifle.

At Union Square in New York City, the crowd demanded justice while a man drew a chalk outline of a body on the brick pavement and added the words "Who's next?"

In Leimert Park, Los Angeles, California, Jackie Vanderbilt and Pat Logan attended a rally and carried a "Demand Justice for Trayvon" poster.

In downtown Miami, demonstrators of diverse ages and races marched with signs in front of the Freedom Tower.

OUTRAGE FROM CELEBRITIES AND PUBLIC OFFICIALS

Sybrina Fulton and Tracy Martin had asked President Barack Obama to look into whether their son's civil rights were violated when GZ stalked and killed him. Not wanting to interfere with a Department of Justice investigation that was being conducted at their request, President Obama limited his comments to saying, "If I had a son, he would look like Trayvon Martin."

Unfortunately, on February 24, 2015, three years after Donald Trump took office, the DOJ closed the investigation. They didn't find enough evidence to pursue federal criminal civil rights charges against George Zimmerman for the fatal shooting of Trayvon Martin. Prosecutors from the Justice Department's Civil Rights Division, officials from the FBI, and the Justice Department's Community Relations Service met with the victim's family and their representatives to explain.

"The death of Trayvon Martin was a devastating tragedy. It shook an entire community, drew the attention of millions across the nation, and sparked a painful but necessary dialogue throughout the country," said Attorney General Eric Holder.

"Though a comprehensive investigation found that the high standard for a federal hate crime prosecution cannot be met under the circumstances here, this young man's premature death necessitates that we continue the dialogue and be unafraid of confronting the issues and tensions his passing brought to the surface. We, as a nation, must take concrete steps to ensure that such incidents do not occur in the future."

Meanwhile, Title 18 of the U.S. Code Section 249 criminalizes willfully causing bodily injury to a person because of that person's actual or perceived race. "Willfully" requires proof that a defendant knew his acts were unlawful and committed those acts in open defiance of the law. This is a very high standard of proof in Florida, where GZ believed the "Stand Your Ground" law gave him the right to kill during a confrontation and claim self-defense.

Considering the federal government's resources, the DOJ should have investigated whether GZ's true motive was to scare his wife or whether he had targeted Trayvon Martin because in the "Stand Your Ground" law courses he took he learned how easy it was to get away with killing a black person in Florida.

REVEREND AL SHARPTON
Pastor, civil rights activist, radio and television commentator

On hearing that GZ was not charged for the slaying of unarmed Trayvon Martin, Reverend Sharpton issued a statement, "There's more than enough probable cause to arrest him. The whole claim of self-defense is bogus. How do you claim self-defense against someone you are pursuing?" He added that it was odd that Zimmerman was a volunteer neighborhood watchman who kept calling 911 to report alleged intruders but attracted no suspicion to himself.

"We have come so far in this country that we can put a black man in the White House, but we can't walk a black child down the neighborhood street to get a bag of Skittles," Reverend Sharpton said. "It is an unbelievable burden, and hard to articulate, that you're born automatically a suspect, and you have to operate and behave in a way that does not exacerbate or incite someone else's paranoia."

The civil rights activist also expressed his disgust that Trayvon Martin's body laid unclaimed in the medical examiner's office before efforts were made to contact his parents.

COREY BOOKER
U.S. Senator from California

"We must mourn the unnecessary & unjust death of a child, but to honor him we must rededicate ourselves to the very ideals that were violated."

JA RULE

Rapper

"Wow so a human life don't mean shit in America… they gave me 2 years for just having a gun."

MICHAEL MOORE

Film producer

"Had a gun-toting Trayvon Martin stalked an unarmed George Zimmerman, and then shot him to death… DO I EVEN NEED TO COMPLETE THIS SENTENCE?"

JAMES VAN DER BEEK

Actor

"Wow, so Florida, when is it not okay to track down and shoot an unarmed teenager?"

RAINN WILSON

Actor

"Hanging out in a gated community with a gun, looking for some suspicious characters today."

MARLON WAYANS

Comedian, actor, producer

"They traded us one OJ and a BARACK for a ZIMMERMAN…So dogs mean more than blacks do in this country. Mike Vick gets two years and Zimmerman gets off? 4give me PETA But this some BULLSHIT! Fuck all of the celebrity! This Black father is appalled and flabbergasted aka pissed fuck off! Damn sad. We bringin slavery back next? I can't even explain this to my kids. How? I'm just gonna put on ROOTS and start from the beginning."

STEVE HARVEY
Television show host, comedian, producer

"A Child is Dead & The Man that Killed Him is Free & Again the Child is Black…My Country Tis of Thee?"

ANDY COHEN
Talk show host, producer

"No Justice"

SEAN DIDDY
Rapper, entrepreneur

"MY PRAYERS GO OUT TO TRAYVONS FAMILY!!!! GOD BLESS THEM!!!!"

DONALD TRUMP

"Zimmerman is no angel but the lack of evidence and the concept of self-defense Especially in Florida law, gave the jury little other choice"

RODDY WHITE
Former wide receiver Atlanta Falcons

"Fucking Zimmerman got away with murder today wow what kind of world do we live in.

"All them jurors should go home tonight and … themselves for letting a grown man get away with killing a kid."

NICKI MINAJ
Rapper

"And our taxes paid for that trial. We just paid to see a murderer walk free after killing an innocent unarmed little boy."

ELIZA DUSHKU
Actor

"Oh man. Just read #Trayvonverdict. My heart goes out to the #Martin family. What a nightmare #tragic."

ELLEN PAGE
Actor

"If u really believe racism isn't a massive problem, that the oppression of minorities is not a horrific and systemic issue. U R in denial."

CHRIS BROWN
Singer

"Bullshit!"

ELLIE GOULDING
Singer and songwriter

"Going to bed with a sober head full of confusion"

JORDIN SPARKS
Singer

"What is happening?!"

SOLANGE KNOWLES
Singer

"Is this not what our ancestors, grandfathers and fathers fought for...? Now I will be fighting for my son..."

NATALIE MAINES
Singer

"Stand Your Ground Law aka, Entrapment."

JOHN CUSACK
Actor

"the need for justice & civil liberties /rights for all Americans inspires US to reclaim rights so this tragedy cld have positive meaning"

NIA VARDALOS
Actor and producer

"Disgusting. This is the second tragic night in the Martin household."

LUPE FIASCO
Actor

"The case should have never been televised as the potential to antagonize US race relations was, in my dumb, opinion too risky & unnecessary"

JENNIFER HUDSON
Singer and actor

"I can't help but think of what my mama used to say 'If u think u seen it all just keep on living'"

MIA FARROW
Actor

"I don't understand this. At ALL"

RICHARD DREYFUSS

Actor

"It's 2013 and an American jury just acquitted a man who admitted to stalking and killing an unarmed child."

JUDY BLUME

Author

"Not surprised. But distraught. Saw 'Fruitvale Station' tonight. How ironic to come home to this verdict."

KATE WALSH

Actor

"Zimmerman verdict sickens me."

KAT DENNINGS

Actor

"I can't handle this. All that really matters are Trayvon's parents, and making sure nothing like this ever happens again."

QUESTLOVE

Musician, author, producer

"This might be in bad taste but in light of this verdict? I really INSIST you people see Fruitvale Station not now but RIGHT NOW"

ALEC BALDWIN

Actor, who recently quit Twitter (again), resurfaced post- verdict

"Florida is a parallel universe. A (expletive) one."

TOM ARNOLD
Actor

"Dear Son, I love you and there is no shame in running away from creepy ass cracker."

MICHAEL IAN BLACK
Actor, comedian, author

"The only thing that surprised me about the verdict is that juries work on Saturdays."

GABRIELLE UNION
Actor

"Help! What's the proper procedure when you're followed by a random armed nutbag returning home from getting candy & iced tea?"

WHOOPI GOLDBERG
Actor and talk show host

"My heart is with Trayvon Martin's family tonight, so my focus is on them. No one else really matters."

JALEEL WHITE
Actor

"I can't ..." wrote the star, adding a sad emoticon to his tweet.

OLIVIA WILDE
Actor and producer

"I feel sick." She then directed a tweet at Ann Coulter, who had tweeted "Hallelujah!" at the verdict. "You are a hateful wench."

MANDY MOORE

Singer and songwriter

"My heart is heavy…for all who knew and loved #TrayvonMartin. His life mattered. This is shameful."

RUSSELL SIMMONS

Businessman and entrepreneur

"I know many people are very upset about the verdict, but we must remain peaceful. No matter what, remain peaceful."

SOPHIA BUSH

Actor director

"The wind is more than knocked out of me… My heart aches for this boy's family. Justice System? I don't think so."

RIHANNA

Singer

"This is the saddest news ever!!!

JOHN LEGEND

Singer and songwriter

"My heart hurts"

LENA DUNHAM

Actor and producer

"No. My heart is with Sybrina Fulton, Rachel Jeantel, everyone who loved Trayvon and has been sent the message that his life didn't matter."

MARIO LOPEZ

Actor

"Hope people don't misbehave after hearing this verdict… Pray for the Martin family."

JOSH GROBAN

Singer

"Oh no. Seriously? Crap."

SHAQUILLE O'NEIL

Former Lakers basketball player and product spokesman

"George Zimmerman not guilty can u believe that. Wow"

MILEY CYRUS

Singer and actor

"No justice. No peace," she wrote, followed by: "The world is a scary place."

12

THE JURORS SPEAK OUT

At the start of the trial Judge Nelson sealed the names of the jurors to shield them from harm. They were assigned the following letters and numbers: B29, B37, B51, B76, E6, and E40.

THE FIRST VOTE WAS SPLIT 3 TO 3

After the forewoman counted the first round of votes, it was a dead heat: 3 to convict and 3 not guilty. Instead of standing their ground, the three who wanted to hold GZ accountable for killing a child were too weak to withstand the bullying from the others.

THEN ONLY TWO JURORS WANTED TO CONVICT

In the movie *12 Angry Men*, Henry Fonda badgered the other 11 jurors until they changed their votes to not guilty. However, in GZ's trial it went the other way. Two jurors told a reporter that their common sense told them not to believe GZ's claim of self-defense. When they tried to persuade the others to change their votes to guilty, they were bullied by the jurors who had lawyers in their families. The two jurors couldn't defend their position because the prosecutors didn't provide them with enough facts to explain to the others why GZ had killed Trayvon that night. And for reasons known only to them, they preferred not to hang the jury. If they had, a different set of prosecutors could have convicted the confessed killer the second time around.

Jurors are also supposed to use their common sense and check out the demeanor of the defendant. In the midst of a whirlwind of evidence and witnesses, GZ was cool and unfazed. To look at him, you could never tell that he had killed a child. Was he a sociopath who killed without conscience or remorse? The voice on the Lauer 911 tape sounded like a kid pleading for his life in horror of a gun being pointed at him. Regardless, GZ and his lawyers twisted it around to say he was the one screaming. Nothing could be more absurd. He was packing a 9 mm Kel-Tec pistol.

Juror B37

This juror said the jury believed that GZ was "good at heart." It brought to mind Anne Frank's diary. Despite the atrocities that had caused her family to hide in an attic, the young girl said she believed their oppressors were "good at heart." Of course, if you had checked back with Anne after her mother and sister were starved and killed in a concentration camp, the girl might have expressed an entirely different opinion of the Nazis.

However, by his own admission in his video statements, what GZ did that rainy night in Sanford contradicted everything the Bible teaches us about good-hearted people. First, he loaded a gun and put an extra bullet in the chamber. Then he got into a car and prowled his neighborhood. When he saw a black teenager, he called 911 and reported him for "being up to no good" just for walking down the street in the rain wearing a hoodie. The operator told him to stop following Trayvon, but he persisted. And when the teenager ducked onto a path behind the buildings to get away from his stalker, GZ jumped out of his car and chased him down on foot. Then he confronted Trayvon with "What are you doing around here?" A struggle ensued, and GZ pulled his gun and shot the unarmed boy through the heart.

For reasons known only to this child killer, GZ called 911 a second time but failed to mention that the child lay dying in the grass. Instead, he posed for pictures of his minor injuries. And when a police officer showed up on the scene, GZ calmly confessed to the dastardly deed, saying he had done it in self-defense.

What was so good-hearted about any of that? It was a total disregard for human life and a display of a depraved heart, proving two elements of second-degree murder. And yet, the prosecutors failed to connect the dots to make these facts their central argument.

The women on the jury who had sat for weeks and heard witness after witness say that GZ had carried a fully loaded weapon with an extra bullet in the chamber the night he had gone looking for trespassers didn't see a problem with any of it. They forgot the typical interviews of neighbors after someone goes berserk and kills somebody. "He was so quiet." "He was such a nice neighbor." Sure, they were, until they snapped.

The juror asked, "Why didn't Trayvon just go home?" Apparently, she slept through the early testimony that showed that the teenager was trying to do that when GZ chased him down. Besides, who wants to lead a molester or other crazy person to their family's home?

Juror B29

This was the only juror of color (who should have known better). She said she believed and trusted Mark O'Mara, the slick defense counsel who gave his best performance in an attempt to collect $400 per hour. Too bad GZ had the last laugh. Like the defendant in *Anatomy of a Murder*, he blew town without paying his legal fees. Poetic justice, I would say. No way they didn't know he was guilty. They gathered witnesses who identified GZ's screams on the 911 tape while it was obviously a much younger voice. GZ's intention was clear in the anger and frustration he exposed to the 911 operator. There was no question about his frame of mind when he chased down and confronted Trayvon. His outrage was rising, not falling.

Juror B37

They misapplied the law. It was clear from statements made by B37, who was married to a lawyer, that the jury ignored Judge Nelson's instructions. Although the defense team had waived "Stand Your Ground" as a justification to exonerate GZ, the jury used it in his favor. It was ingrained in Florida culture and they didn't understand that it cut both ways. After he was stalked and confronted, Trayvon also had the right to stand his ground. Regardless of this fact and every other fact against GZ that proved the neighborhood watchman was on a mission to make an example of this black intruder, the jurors gave him every benefit of the doubt.

This juror claimed that there was no evidence to prove that GZ was guilty. This was true at all. They had a lot of facts, including GZ's video statements that were filled with lies and contradictions. They could have chosen not to discard them. Instead, they decided to believe him and then justified it by saying they had no choice.

Juror B37 went so far as to blame Trayvon for his own killing. "He could have gone home." This, of course, was what he was trying to do when he was chased down. Applying her logic, GZ could have stayed in his car and obeyed the instructions of the 911 operator to stop following the teenager. While GZ claimed that Trayvon was "acting suspicious," the teenager was just distracted while talking to Rachel Jeantel on his cell phone.

It was unfair for the jurors to b lame Trayvon. It was the prosecutors' fault they didn't get it right. They dropped the ball from the opening statement through the closing arguments and their sorry efforts let Trayvon's family and the whole country down.

An Anonymous Juror

A juror who preferred to remain anonymous believed that Trayvon was peeking in windows. Would she have jumped to the same conclusion if it had been a white kid? Although GZ might have been overzealous, he had approached the kid in good faith to protect the neighborhood. She bought his story that he was a 208-pound weakling and found all the defense witnesses more believable than the prosecution's, especially Rachel Jeantel. Although she lacked credibility, the juror believed her when she told them that Trayvon had called GZ "a creepy ass cracker." Otherwise, the anonymous juror said she didn't understand the rest of what Trayvon's friend said. That, of course, was the prosecutors' fault for not properly preparing Rachel for cross-examination.

While Juror B37 believed Rachel Jeantel when she said Trayvon called GZ "a creepy ass cracker," she chose not to believe the rest of the girls' testimony. For example, Rachel said that she heard GZ confront Trayvon with "What are you doing around here?" Trayvon responded, "Get off!" and then the teenager's cell phone went silent.

The juror also thought GZ wasn't a racist. The Grand Wizards of the Klan also denied that they were racists. They just wanted the white race to stay pure. Somebody should clue them in that it's too late. Rarely would any American citizen's DNA test prove their ancestry was entirely European. The mixing of races started long ago after Lucy's descendants had ventured out of Africa. She was the first modern human's remains that have been found.

All Six Jurors

They claimed that race was not a factor in their verdict. Considering the exclusion of black people from their lives and the negative images of black people in the South as being lazy or violent, how could race not have anything to do with it?

13

CRAZY STUFF

THAT HAPPENED NEXT

GZ MOCKED THE TRIAL, TRIED TO SELL HIS GUN, AND PLANNED A BOXING MATCH WITH DMX

GZ went to gun shows trying to sell the gun he used to kill Trayvon Martin. As if that wasn't shameless enough, he contacted boxing promoter Damon Feldman, who set up a match with rapper DMX with one of thousands of opponents he considered to fight the confessed killer for a million dollar payday.

Rapper DMX had said, "I am going to beat the living f**k out of him. I am breaking every rule in boxing to make sure I f**k him up right." DMX added that he would also urinate on Zimmerman's face, something millions were eager to watch.

On August 8, 2014, depriving them of the pleasure to witness the beatdown, the promoter cancelled it on Twitter, "It was my decision to cancel the George Zimmerman fight; it was worth a lot of money to me but people's feelings meant more to me."

The idea of GZ in a boxing match with anyone is outrageous and contradicts the way he portrayed himself during the murder trial as being too cowardly to fight back to save his life against a 17-year-old kid who weighed 60 pounds less than him. However, he wasn't too scared to pull out his 9 mm Kel-Tec semi-automatic pistol and blow the kid away.

GZ THREATENED TO FEED JAY-Z TO FLORIDA ALLIGATORS

Based on the books Rest in Power: The Enduring Life of Trayvon Martin by Trayvon Martin's parents, Sybrina Fulton and Tracy Martin, and Suspicion Nation: The Inside Story of the Trayvon Martin Injustice and Why We Continue to Repeat It by Lisa Bloom, Jay-Z and The Weinstein Company produced a six-part documentary about the killing of Trayvon Martin.

When Jay-Z's production crew approached GZ's family for a statement, the confessed killer became enraged that they were making a film about how he got away with murder. The confessed killer threatened to feed Jay-Z to the Florida alligators. "Hold-up!" cried Snoop Dogg. "If one hair on Jay's hair is touched, that's when the revolution will be televised.

We one, and thank the system let the Bitch ass muthaf***a get away with murder—try it again!" Before GZ's trial, Shellie claimed she and GZ were so terrified they hid in the woods in a 20-foot trailer. Now how scared was GZ that Snoop Dogg's many hip-hop fans would come after him?

Snoop ended his Instagram rant with, "Trayvon Martin Gone but not forgotten." Meanwhile, GZ keeps getting into disputes with strangers while wearing a bulletproof vest. Too bad Trayvon didn't have one.

14

RESPONSE TO MORE KILLINGS AND ACQUITTALS: VOTE THEM OUT!

SPECIAL PROSECUTOR ANGELA COREY LOST HER TRY FOR RE-ELECTION

In August 2016, three years after her team was responsible for GZ's acquittal, Special Prosecutor Angela Corey got her comeuppance when she lost her bid for reelection to fellow Republican Melissa Nelson. During her term as the Florida state prosecutor, Corey was overzealous at the wrong times. While she ruthlessly put Marissa Alexander, a 31-year-old black woman, in prison for 20 years for firing a warning shot over her husband's head to stop his domestic violence, Corey's efforts to lock up GZ for killing Trayvon Martin were listless at best and negligent at worst.

IN MEMORY OF LAQUAN MCDONALD: BYE-BYE, ANITA ALVAREZ

In October 2014, Chicago Police Officer Jason Van Dyke shot 17-year-old Laquan McDonald 16 times. The release of the video in November sparked massive protests. However, a year went by before Cook County Prosecutor Anita Alvarez charged Van Dyke with murder.

"I have been criticized that I wasn't a very good politician…But I am very damn proud of the fact that I am a good prosecutor," Alvarez said.

But she didn't prove it when she botched the trial of Laquan's killer and Officer Van Dyke was acquitted.

Outraged Chicagoans organized protests and a voter drive. Following their defeat of Alvarez in her bid for reelection, Assata's Daughters, Black Lives Matter, Chicago, BYP100, and Fearless Leading by the Youth released a joint statement:

"The #ByeAnita campaign celebrated last night. Not because Kim Foxx won (by 52.21 percent of the vote) but because Anita Alvarez lost. Due to her essential role in the cover-up of Laquan McDonald's murder, young black organizers relentlessly targeted Alvarez's campaign for re-election in the final weeks. Not because we support Kim Foxx (in the Democratic Primary), but because Anita Alvarez is a prosecutor who has demonstrated that she does not believe black lives matter. When we began to target Alvarez's campaign she was ahead of her opponents in the polls. Last night, we saw the fruits of our labor manifest as Anita Alvarez conceded the Cook County state's attorney race."

In the general election, the finger power of the outraged citizens swept Democrat Foxx into office for Cook County's top prosecutor against Republican Christopher Pfannkuche. Foxx, who was more responsive to the interests of the black community, was put in charge of 800 attorneys and 1,500 employees.

IN MEMORY OF TAMIR RICE: SO LONG, TIMOTHY MCGINTY

Cleveland, Ohio citizens were extremely dissatisfied with how Prosecutor Timothy McGinty handled the November 22, 2014 shooting of 12-year old Tamir Rice by Police Officer Timothy Loehmann. The saying goes that a grand jury would indict a cheese sandwich if a prosecutor asked them to.

However, McGinty failed to recommend charges against Loehmann or his partner, Officer Frank Garmback, for excessive force when they arrived at the Cudell Rec Center and Loehmann shot the child who was playing with a toy pellet gun. Tamir died the following day.

His mother, Samaria Rice, loudly criticized McGinty and accused him of mishandling the case and failing to advocate on behalf of her son. The prosecutor shot back, "They have their own economic motives." Instead of silently stewing, the Rice family took action. They gathered more than 100,000 signatures on a petition to remove McGinty from office. When he refused to go, they mounted a "vote him out" campaign and defeated the Cuyahoga County prosecutor in the 2016 Democratic Primary, where he lost to Michael O'Malley.

IN MEMORY OF ERIC GARNER: GOODBYE, DAN DONOVAN

In July 2014, after Police Officer Daniel Pentaleo killed Eric Garner with a chokehold in the New York City borough of Staten Island, Al Sharpton declared that Lady Justice was choked too. He was right. Under public pressure, Dan Donovan, the district attorney, reluctantly filed murder charges with the grand jury. However, they refused to indict the cop, and Donovan refused to allow the transcripts of the hearing to be released to the public. Garner's last words, "I can't breathe," sparked a movement, and the Garner family and activists protested the cover-up.

Fortunately, Donovan voluntarily left office to run for Congress. Although he was endorsed by Donald Trump and won, his victory was short-lived. In November 2018, Staten Island voters rejected his bid for reelection and replaced him with Democrat Max Rose.

IN MEMORY OF MICHAEL BROWN: BOB MCCULLOCH IS DEFEATED

On August 9, 2014, only a month after Eric Garner was brutally killed by a cop, unarmed 18-year old Michael Brown was shot down in Ferguson, Missouri by Police Officer Darren Wilson. Despite organized protests, the grand jury refused to indict him.

The prosecutor, Bob McCulloch, had been in office 27 years, and he ignored the Garner family's cries for justice.

But they did not sit idly by. With friends and neighbors, they marched and shouted their concerns for the world to hear. They sparked the "Color of Change" and "Black Lives Matter" movements that have spread across the country.

Finally, in 2018, Prosecutor McCullough felt the heat for failing to enforce the law against cold-blooded murder when Wesley Bell, a young African American reformer who ran a campaign fueled by a coalition of local and national organizers, defeated him in the Democratic Primary and won in the general election.

In 2019, Brown's father asked Bell to reopen the investigation into his son's murder and sent a petition to the governor of Missouri. "McCulloch completely ignored standard protocol for a Prosecuting Attorney…and it was a setup from the beginning." In a separate statement, Color of Change President Rashad Robinson said, "We stand with…tens of thousands of (our) members demanding that Missouri Governor Mike Parson reopen the investigation into the fatal shooting of Mike Brown."

15

ADVICE TO BLACK YOUTH

When a police officer or a stranger approaches you in a menacing way while you are on your cell phone, have the person you're talking to call 911 to summon help. If you have a smart phone, start recording. If you have a phone or not, say, "Sir, I'm not resisting." Then slowly raise both hands high in the air and ask, "May I please have a lawyer?" Never confront a mob or anyone you don't know.

In 1955, Mamie Till sent her 14-year-old son, Emmett, from Chicago to rural Mississippi to spend his summer holiday with family. As she packed, she explained how a black youth should conduct himself in the South. "If you have to, get on your knees and bow when a white person goes past," she told him. "Be humble and do it willingly."

"Okay, Mama," Emmett said, humoring her. No way he was going to kiss anybody's ass. After all, he won his share of fights on the streets of Chicago. And while he never looked for trouble, he could take care of himself no matter what color the folks were.

And so, when the teen from the hood was confronted by racists in the small town of Money, Mississippi, he failed to heed his mother's warning and behaved like he was at home. He said, "bye, baby" or whistled at a pretty white woman in a grocery store. Retaliation came swiftly that night when a mob dragged him out of bed.

Three days later, the body of Mamie Till's son was fished out of the Tallahatchie River. The coroner found Emmett's head crushed, a bullet in his skull, and one of his eyes gouged out.

In small Southern towns like Money, Mississippi, everybody knows who did what, when and where, and to whom. Especially when they went around bragging like the Chicago boy's killers did. Although they were arrested, an all-white jury found the men not guilty within an hour. "If we hadn't stopped to drink pop," a juror boasted, "it wouldn't have taken that long!"

The acquittal of these brutal murderers created a sensation in the black press. Mrs. Till insisted that *Jet* magazine show a picture of her son's bloated and mutilated body on its cover for the world to see. Toni Morrison responded with a play, Langston Hughes wrote a poem, and Bob Dylan penned a song about the outrageous crime.

Just three months later, when Rosa Parks refused to give up her seat in Montgomery, Alabama, she claimed the outrageous execution of Emmett Till was on her mind and compelled her to do something. It didn't shame his killers who spoke brazenly in a national magazine. Allegedly, they were just trying to scare the boy, but when the Chicagoan refused to beg for mercy, they "had to kill him to keep uppity blacks in their place."

Sixty-four years passed following the atrocity. Then last year (2019), Emmett Till was in the news again. Racists traveled to Illinois where they defaced Emmett's headstone and stomped on his grave.

16

BREAKING THE LAWYERS' CODE
OF SILENCE

Lawyers have something in common with doctors and mobsters: a code of silence. It keeps us from ratting each other out when we screw up. But this author can no longer tolerate the conspiracy within the legal community to look every direction except at the awful truth: that our Florida colleagues participated in a farce with the trial of George Zimmerman, the confessed killer of Trayvon Martin.

Prosecutors like me watched the shoddy performance of these prosecutors in disbelief as they set the killer free. Afterwards, they nonchalantly went about their business and denied any responsibility that they had set a cold-blooded killer free. After the not guilty verdict, where were the shouts of outrage? Prosecutors across the country should have stood up and denounced the failure of Corey's team to fight for the truth, the whole truth, and nothing but the truth.

My book *A Million Prosecutor Mistakes: How They Lost the Trial of Trayvon Martin's Confessed Killer (George Zimmerman)* is the first in a series of exposes that I plan to write about the misconduct of my fellow lawyers. My purpose is to expose them to the court of public opinion. Dear reader, that's your court! This is where each citizen can demand justice and take whatever action is necessary to change what's wrong with our legal system.

As explained in an earlier chapter, prosecutors can't be sued for malpractice by the victim's family. According to laws written by lawyers, thousands of prosecutors across the country are immune from civil lawsuits and can't be held accountable for their lame performances except by the court of public opinion. When they fail to act in the best interests of your community, you must use the power of your finger and vote them out of office.

Get mad as hell and refuse to take it anymore when your elected officials don't care enough to get justice for your community and convict the George Zimmermans who go around slaying your children. Your men and women too! Use your index finger in the booth to get rid of prosecutors who fail to meet the needs of your community. Stop putting up with prosecutors and their assistant prosecutors who only pretend to be prosecutors and assistant prosecutors. Select and support your own candidates from your neighborhoods who will protect your rights. President Barack Obama showed everybody how to run a grassroots campaign. He raised money on the internet and formed a coalition of Hispanics, blacks, and whites who cared enough about real change to contribute and vote for him because he cared.

What about you, dear reader? Do you truly care? Do you care enough to do something to bring about change in your local legal system?

APPENDIX

---

i.

UPDATE TO FLORIDA
"STAND YOUR GROUND" LAW

In 2005, the Florida Legislature passed the "Stand Your Ground" law. It allowed a person who believed their life was in danger to use deadly force and imposed no duty on them to retreat from a dangerous situation. Because self-defense is considered an affirmative defense and a killer is required to prove beyond a reasonable doubt that there was an imminent threat to his life, it was baffling that the GZ prosecutors waived its application during pretrial motions in the case.

Several years later, as if "Stand Your Ground" didn't make it easy enough to get away with murder, Florida legislators took the burden off of the killer to prove he had acted in self-defense and imposed it on the prosecutors to disprove it at a pretrial hearing. Because of the presumption of innocence, the new law is a field day for vigilantes and a windfall for criminal attorneys who can collect high fees and avoid lengthy trials.

Fortunately, at least one Florida Circuit Court saw through the Legislature's attempt to legalize murder. Miami-Dade Judge Milton Hirsch ruled that revisions to the "Stand Your Ground" law were procedural, meaning the state supreme court had the sole right to enact them.

Meanwhile, the other circuit courts stand ready to provide get out of jail free cards to cold-blooded killers with a "shoot first" mentality. Of course, the public defenders and the National Rifle Association have praised the new law, while the Florida Prosecuting Attorneys Association and gun control advocates oppose it. "Every battery case, every domestic violence case, every use of force case, as a matter of routine, defense attorneys will now request hearings," said Phil Archer, a state attorney.

A recent study published in the *Journal of the American Medical Association* found that Florida's implementation of the contested law resulted in a 31.6 percent increase in gun-related homicides. "Who will speak for the victims who have forever been silenced by an aggressor who falsely claims he wasn't an aggressor but is protected by a flawed law?" asked Florida's Democratic Representative Bobby Dubose.

ii.

LEGAL WORDS AND PHRASES

AFFIRMATIVE DEFENSE, usually found in a lesser included offense with the primary charge that requires a defendant to prove the elements listed in the statute beyond a reasonable doubt

ARRAIGNMENT, a court proceeding where a suspect enters a plea of guilty, not guilty, or no contest to a crime

ARREST, a suspect is charged with a crime and taken into police custody

ASKED AND ANSWERED, according to the rules of evidence and criminal procedure, it's an objection made by the opponent's counsel that the question has previously been asked and answered by a witness on the stand

CHAIN OF CUSTODY, the record of who has handled the evidence taken from a crime scene until the day it was presented at a court proceeding

CIRCUMSTANTIAL EVIDENCE, the other evidence used where the suspect was not caught in the act of committing a crime

CLOSING ARGUMENTS, persuasive statements made by the lawyers to the judge or jury after they have rested their cases that explain the evidence that proves the defendant was guilty or not guilty of a crime

CROSS-EXAMINATION, questions asked to a witness on the stand by the opponent's counsel in an effort to contradict, impeach, and destroy his credibility

DIRECT EXAMINATION, questions asked to a witness on the stand by counsel on the same side of the case

DOUBLE JEOPARDY, a legal right that bars any person from being put on trial twice for the same offense for which they had already been found not guilty

ELEMENTS OF THE CRIME, the specific circumstances a prosecutor is required by a criminal statute to prove beyond a reasonable doubt that a defendant has committed a crime

EVIDENCE, documents, video presentations, or testimony by a witness intended to prove a fact in dispute at the trial

FOUNDATION, the rules of evidence and criminal procedure require the individual who made the statement or other proof to testify in court to identify it, explain the circumstances of how it was made, and be subjected to cross-examination by opposing counsel

HEARSAY, an out-of-court statement that must be excluded from evidence because it was not subjected to cross-examination by the opponent's counsel

HOMICIDE, the killing of a human being by another

JURY INSTRUCTIONS, the rules of law that a judge tells the jury that they must apply to the facts they decide are true in order to convict or acquit a defendant of a crime

LAYING A FOUNDATION, OR THE PROPER FOUNDATION, all evidence presented at trial must meet the requirements of being relevant to the case under the rules of evidence, criminal procedures, and other laws. No witness is qualified to testify about any matter unless that person has personal knowledge of the facts, and no document can be presented to the court without identifying who had created it, and when and where it was kept. Also, the witness identifying the evidence must be the person who created it, witnessed it being created, or was the custodian of it.

LESSER INCLUDED OFFENSE, a charge that comes with a lesser sentence and is added to the primary charge, e.g., manslaughter is charged with second-degree murder

MANSLAUGHTER, under Florida criminal law, prosecutors had to prove the following three elements beyond a reasonable doubt:

1. That Trayvon Martin was killed.
2. That GZ was negligent or accidentally killed Trayvon.

3. That killing Trayvon was not excused or justifiable by law.

MOTION IN LIMINE, a lawyer files a motion to limit or exclude evidence that the other side wants to submit to the court

MURDER, the unlawful killing of a human being by another as determined by a judge or jury in a court proceeding

OBJECTION, a loud protest by a lawyer in court against a question, evidence, or procedure for violating the law or procedure

OPENING STATEMENT, an argument made to the judge or jury that explains the evidence that will be submitted during the trial to prove the defendant is guilty or not guilty

PRIMA FACIE CASE, the elements of a crime or a defense listed in a statute that must be proven to find a defendant guilty

SECOND CHAIR, a lawyer who assists the primary lawyer in a court proceeding

SECOND-DEGREE MURDER, under Florida criminal law, these are the five elements of the crime that the prosecution had to prove:

1. That Trayvon Martin was killed.
2. That Trayvon Martin was killed by GZ.
3. That when GZ killed Trayvon Martin, he was committing another crime.
4. That killing Trayvon was not excusable or justifiable by law.
5. That when GZ killed Trayvon Martin he was depraved and showed no regard for human life.

WITNESS PREP OR PREPARATION, a lawyer reviews the evidence with a witness to help them understand and properly answer the questions that will be asked of them by both sides during a trial

WITNESSES, persons who appear and give evidence under oath in a court proceeding

GEORGE ZIMMERMAN'S FORTY-SIX 911 CALLS

GZ made dozens of calls to the police in the years before he killed Trayvon Martin.

Along with the audio recordings of *six calls* to Sanford police that GZ made in the weeks before the February 26 shooting of Trayvon Martin, the Sanford Police Department posted *reports* of 46 calls to 911's nonemergency line that GZ made between August 2004 and February26, 2012 the day he shot and killed Trayvon Martin.

Below is the list *The Daily Beast* compiled of the calls from the dispatcher's reports. Verbatim excerpts of the reports appear in quotes.

General Terms:
TEL = non-911 police number (answered by 911 dispatcher)
BM = black male
LSW = last seen wearing

The calls are listed here in reverse order starting from GZ's second call to 911 right after he had shot and killed Trayvon Martin:

46. February 26, 2012 – 7:20 p.m. Type: TEL
Subject: Suspicious activity Report: Repeats prior report

45. February 26, 2012 (night of Trayvon Martin shooting)
– 7:11 p.m. Type: TEL
Subject: Suspicious activity
Report: Black male "late teens lsw dark gray hoodie jeans or sweatpants walking around area"…"subj now running towards back entrance of complex"

44. February 2, 2012 – 8:29 p.m. Type: TEL
Subject: Suspicious activity
Report: "BM lsw: black leather jacket, black hat, printed PJ pants, he keeps going to this location"

43. January 29, 2012 – 5:38 p.m. Type: TEL
Subject: Disturbance
Report: Children "running and playing in the street"

42. December 10, 2011 – 5:29 p.m. Type: TEL
Subject: Disturbance
Report: "At the club house"…"Male subject [arrived on scene] that thought he was employed by" Zimmerman…"Subj is expected to get paid for serving food."…Zimmerman "said that he didn't wish him to serve at the [event]"…Zimmerman "hired someone else, subj sounded upset and wants to get paid"

41. October 1, 2011 – 12:53 a.m. Type: TEL
Subject: Suspicious activity
Report: Two black male suspects "20–30 YOA in [white] Chevy poss Impala at the gate of the community." Zimmerman "does not recognize subjs or veh and is concerned due to recent" burglaries in the area

40. September 23, 2011 – 11:08 p.m. Type: TEL
Subject: Neighbor/Suspicious activity
Report: Zimmerman reports "open garage door"…Describes "neighborhood watch mtg last night with Sgt Herx who [advised] to report anything [suspicious]"…Zimmerman "is part of neighborhood watch" and is concerned because of recent burglaries in the area

39. August 6, 2011 – 10:20 p.m.
Type: TEL
Subject: Suspicious activity
Report: Two black males, one wearing a black tank top and black shorts, the second wearing a black t-shirt and jeans…"Subjs are in their teens"

38. August 3, 2011 – 6:45 p.m.
Type: TEL
Subject: Suspicious activity
Report: Black male last seen wearing a white tank top and black shorts… Zimmerman "believes subject is involved in recent" burglaries in the neighborhood

37. May 27, 2011 – 9:18 a.m.
Type: TEL Subject: Alarm
Report: Zimmerman "has a self-responding alarm that just notified him of" an alarm at this location

36. April 22, 2011 – 7:09 p.m.
Type: TEL
Subject: Suspicious activity
Report: Juvenile black male "apprx 7–9" years old, four feet tall "skinny build short blk hair" last seen wearing a blue t-shirt and blue shorts

35. March 18, 2011 – 9:26 p.m.
Type: 911 Subject: Animals
Report: Zimmerman requested an officer meet him regarding a pit bull in his garage

34. November 26, 2010 – 2:54 a.m. Type: TEL
Subject: Alarm
Report: Zimmerman was out of town and a motion alarm he monitors himself went off

33. November 8, 2010 – 6:54 p.m. Type: TEL
Subject: Maintenance
Report: Zimmerman reports "trash in roadwy"

32. October 2, 2010 – 1:55 p.m. Type: TEL
Subject: Disturbance
Report: Zimmerman reports "blu jeep grand Cherokee female driver yelling at elderly passengers…windows are

tinted"…"the veh was rocking back and forth and he could hear the female yelling"

31. June 26, 2010 – 11:00 p.m.
Type: 911
Subject: Disturbance
Report: "Loud party…approx 50 subjs & blocking the street"

30. June 12, 2010 – 11:13 p.m.
Type: 911
Subject: Disturbance
Report: Subject "at the clubhouse & pool areas having a party"

29. April 28, 2010 – 9:02 p.m.
Type: TEL
Subject: Disturbance
Report: "White older model four-door Buick or Oldsmobile" obstructing road

28. February 27, 2010 – 4:46 p.m. Type: TEL
Subject: Suspicious activity
Report: "Residence w/a lot of [suspicious] activity"…"multiple vehs are constantly coming to the" location…"punk subs run out to the vehs and run back inside"…"the subjs are always outside w/the garage open"…"the subjs hang out towards the st all night//ongoing problem"

27. January 12, 2010 – 10:25 p.m.
Type: TEL Subject: Neighbor
Report: Open garage door…Zimmerman says "this is very unlike his neighbor"…"there is a lot of electronics in the resd and posb in the garage"

26. January 1, 2010 – 4:34 a.m.
Type: 911
Subject: Disturbance
Report: Zimmerman reports reckless driver in "purplish Ford Ranger single cab"

25. November 3, 2009 – 5:04 p.m. Type: TEL
Subject: Disturbance
Report: White Ford F350 that was "cutting people off"

24. November 21, 2009 – 2:26 p.m.
Type: 911 Subject: Unclear

23. October 23, 2009 – 9:18 a.m. Type: TEL
Subject: Animals
Report: "Aggressive white and brown pitbull" sitting outside Zimmerman's home

22. September 22, 2009 – 6:00 p.m.
Type: 911
Subject: Disturbance
Report: "Yellow speed bike … was speeding and weaving in and out of traffic and doing wheelies"

21. September 7, 2009 – 9:01 p.m. Type: TEL
Subject: Maintenance
Report: "Pothole in the road" … "it is deep and can cause damage to vehicles"

20. August 26, 2009 – 8:35 p.m. Type: TEL
Subject: Suspicious activity
Report: "Gold Caprice…male driving with no headlights…speeding"

19. Aug. 21, 2009 – 6:57 p.m.
Type: TEL Subject: Conflict

Report: "Landlord is trying to take [Zimmerman's] money for rent...and home in foreclosure"

18. June 16, 2009 – 3:50 p.m.
Type: TEL
Subject: Disturbance
Report: Persons in the pool area playing basketball, "jumpin over the fence going into pool area and trashin the bathroom"

17. June 10, 2009 – 1:55 a.m.
Type: 911 Subject: Alarm
Report: Fire alarm going off

16. May 4, 2009 – 4:07 p.m.
Type: TEL
Subject: Suspicious activity Report: Reports a blue Audi A4

15. March 12, 2009 – 6:58 p.m.
Type: TEL Subject: Patrol
Report: Patrol request between March 13 and March 22

14. January 5, 2009 – 10:53 p.m.
Type: 911 Subject: Alarm
Report: Fire alarm going off

13. November 25, 2007 – 12:40 a.m. Type: TEL
Subject: Disturbance
Report: "Ex roommate is letting people that [Zimmerman] don't like in the" house

12. November 25, 2007 – 12:21 a.m.
Type: 911
Subject: Disturbance

Report: White male ex-roommate last seen wearing a red Florida State University shirt

11. October 14, 2007 – 4:10 p.m. Type: TEL
Subject: Suspicious activity
Report: Possible criminal mischief to the tire of Zimmerman's black Dodge Durango

10. June 24, 2007 – 12:48 a.m.
Type: TEL
Subject: Suspicious activity
Report: "By the pool," two Hispanic males and one white male with "slim jim"

9. November 4, 2006 – 2:37 a.m. Type: TEL
Subject: Suspicious activity
Report: A call regarding a "late model red" Toyota pickup "driving around the neighborhood and apt complex for the past 5 min"

8. September 23, 2005 – 7:03 p.m.
Type: 911
Subject: Suspicious activity
Report: Zimmerman's "little sister just call him from above" his address and advises "there was a" suspicious person "at the front door"

7. September 21, 2005 – 9:00 p.m.
Type: 911 Subject: Animals
Report: Reports a stray dog

6. April 27, 2005 – 12:40 a.m.
Type: 911 Subject: Neighbor
Report: Open garage door

5. March 17, 2005 – 7:21 p.m.
Type: 911

Subject: Maintenance
Report: Pothole "that is blocking the road"

4. October 20, 2004 – 9:13 p.m.
Type: 911
Subject: Disturbance
Report: Drunk pedestrian walking in the road

3. August 20, 2004 – 11:33 p.m.
Type: 911 Subject: Neighbor
Report: Reports an open garage door

2. August 12, 2004 – 10:03 a.m.
Type: 911
Subject: Suspicious activity Report: Repeats earlier report

1. August 12, 2004 – 9:59 a.m.
Type: 911
Subject: Suspicious activity
Report: Places a call reporting a male in a green Ford pickup

iv.

RESOURCES

Dear Reader,

While this author has primarily relied on her experience as a lawyer, including 4 years as a magistrate and 29 years as a prosecutor, and on the continuing legal education courses required annually by the Ohio Supreme Cour that were hosted by the Lorain County Bar Association, the Ohio State Bar Association, and Lawline, for your convenience, every effort was made to place most of the supplemental reference materials used to write this book in the same order as the relevant chapters. Of course, the topics are not exclusive to any particular chapter and by necessity will overlap.

INTRO: WHY I WROTE THIS BOOK

April 13, 2012 issue of People Magazine, page 60, "An American Tragedy: Heartbreaking New Details"

CNN's live coverage of George Zimmerman's trial June 2013–July 13, 2013   Fox News' live coverage of George Zimmerman's trial June 2013–July 13, 2013 HLN's live coverage of George Zimmerman's trial June 2013–July 13, 2013

MSNBC's live coverage of George Zimmerman's trial June 2013–July 13, 2013 George Zimmerman ("Trayvon Martin") Trial (2013) famous-trials.com/zimmerman1

The Zimmerman Trial, Day by Day – NYTimes.com
archive.nytimes.com/www.nytimes.com/interactive/2013/07/12/us/zimmerman- highlights.html

The Curious Case of Trayvon Martin:
nytimes.com/2012/03/17/opinion/blow-the-curious-case-of-Trayvon-Martin.html

George Zimmerman sues Trayvon Martin's family for 100 million dollars bbc.com/news/newsbeat-50671843

CHAPTER 1: KILLING TRAYVON MARTIN

George Zimmerman on trial in death of Fla. teen – Photo 18 … cbsnews.com/pictures/george-zimmerman-on-trial-in-death-of-fla-teen/18

The Facts in the Zimmerman Trial | The New Yorker newyorker.com/news/daily-comment/the-facts-in-the-zimmerman-trial July 16, 2013

Linton, Caroline (15 July 2013) The Daily Beast, "Who Is Angela Corey? From Being Fired to Prosecuting Zimmerman"

thebradfordreview.blogspot.com/2012/06/governor-rick-scott-fl-announces-new.html Gov. Scott Announces "Stand Your Ground" Task Force

wctv.tv/home/headlines/Gov_Scott_Announces_Stand_Your_Ground_Task_Force_14 8104835.html,
tampabay.com/news/politics/gubernatorial/gov-rick-scott-appoints-special-prosecutor- for-trayvon-martin-case/1221406

Bridget Murphy, "Shorstein dismisses longtime assistant", Florida Times-Union,
November 17, 2006

foxnews.com/world/new-photo-shows-bloody-george-zimmerman-allegedly-on-night- of-trayvon-martin-shooting

news.yahoo.com/2013/12/13/ap-photos-zimmerman-trial-gunshot-jury-184242981.html

Trayvon Martin Shooter told cops teenager went for his gun abcnews.go.com/US/Trayvon-Martin-shooter-teenager-gun/story?id=16000239 March 25, 2012, 11:03 PM

Yamiche Alcindor, "Zimmerman held pending arraignment in Trayvon shooting," USA TODAY April 12, 2012

Jeff Weiner, "Dershowitz: Zimmerman prosecutor ranted against Harvard" (FL)
The Orlando Sentinel 6 June, 2012

Trayvon Martin Shooting Fast Facts
cnn.com/2013/06/05/us/Trayvon-Martin-shooting-fast-facts/index.html

CHAPTER 2: THE PUBLIC DEMANDS JUSTICE

cbsnews.com/pictures/nationwide-protests-over-Trayvon-Martin-case/
Retrieved September 2, 2013

Trayvon Martin's death: the story so far
theguardian.com/world/2012/mar/20/Trayvon-Martin-death-story-so-far
theguardian.com/world/2012/mar/31/Trayvon-Martin-protest-march-sanford

Trayvon Martin and the Irony of American Justice
theatlantic.com/national/archive/2013/07/Trayvon-Martin-and-the-irony-of-american-justice/277782

NAACP Townhall calls for justice for Trayvon Martin
naacp.org/latest/naacp-townhall-calls-for-justice-for-Trayvon-Martin/
Justice for Trayvon Martin Updated March 22, 2012

Urban League of Portland ulpdx.org/news_/justice-for-Trayvon-Martin/
July 15, 2013

Trayvon Martin case: Rev. Al Sharpton takes civil rights stage
latimes.com/nation/la-xpm-2012-mar-22-la-na-nn-Trayvon-Martin-case-rev-al- sharpton-20120322-story.html

Al Sharpton plays several sides in Trayvon Martin story ...
washingtonpost.com/lifestyle/style/2013/07/19/03edafe2-efd5-11e2-
9008- 61e94a7ea20d_story.html
July 19, 2013

Justice for Trayvon Martin thenation.com/article/justice-Trayvon-
Martin/ By Mychal Denzel Smith. March 19, 2012

CHAPTER 3: GZ IS CHARGED WITH SECOND-DEGREE MURDER

Democracy Now! 04/2012 "45 Days After Killing Trayvon Martin &
Sparking National Outcry, George Zimmerman Finally Charged,"
democracynow.org

CNN Wire Staff. "Experts argue appropriateness of murder charge in
Martin case,"
CNN April 12, 2012, accessed April 13, 2012

"Harvard Law prof: Charges against Zimmerman won't hold up"
Hardball With Chris Matthews. MSNBC. Retrieved 13 April 2012.

Reuters. "Trayvon Martin's killer showed signs of injury: neighbors,"
Reuters April 16, 2012, accessed April 19, 2012.

Emily S. Rueb, The New York Times, "First Florida White Man in 30
years is sentenced to die for killing a black man", April 25, 2019

Susan Taylor, The Tampa Bay Times, "Florida 'stand your ground' law
yields some shocking outcomes depending on how law is applied".
Feb. 17, 2013

A former police officer in Florida was sentenced Thursday to 25 years
in prison for fatally shooting a black man who had been awaiting help
on a highway more than three years ago

"Zimmerman charged with second-degree murder" Politics Nation with Al Sharpton. MSNBC. Retrieved 21 April 2012.

Jeff Weiner, "Dershowitz: Zimmerman prosecutor ranted against Harvard", Orlando Sentinel,
June 6, 2012.

George Zimmerman Charged With 2nd Degree Murder in Trayvon …
abcnews.go.com/US/george-zimmerman-charged…
Apr 11, 2012

George Zimmerman charged with second-degree murder in …
washingtonpost.com/politics/george-zimmerman-to-be-charged-in-Trayvon… April 11, 2012

Zimmerman booked on 2nd-degree murder charge - CBS News
cbsnews.com/news/zimmerman-booked-on-2nd-degree-murder-charge
Jul 10, 2013

Zimmerman charged with 2nd-degree murder in Trayvon Martin …
news4jax.com/news/local/zimmerman-charged-with-2nd-degree-murder April 12, 2012

Huckabee, Mike. Dershowitz: Zimmerman Special Prosecutor Angela Corey Should Be Disbarred, Real Clear Politics, July 14, 2013

CHAPTER 4: MEET THE JUDGE, PROSECUTORS, AND DEFENSE TEAMS

The Judge

4th Judicial Circuit Court – Welcome jud4.org

Trial of George Zimmerman – Wikipedia
en.wikipedia.org/wiki/State_of_Florida_v._George_Zimmerman

Debra Steinberg Nelson – Ballotpedia
ballotpedia.org/Debra_Steinberg_Nelson

Meet the new judge in Zimmerman case, Debra Nelson
mynews13.com/fl/orlando/news/2012/8/30/zimmerman_judge_debr
August 30, 2012

Judge Debra Nelson: They Loved Her for the Zimmerman Trial …
huffpost.com/entry/judge-debra-nelson-george-zimmerman-
trial_b_3581657 September 10, 2013

sao4th.com/about/meet-mrs-nelson-and-her-team

The Prosecutors

Who Is Angela Corey? From Being Fired to Prosecuting Zimmerman
thedailybeast.com/who-is-angela-corey-from-being-fired-to-
prosecuting…   Caroline Linton Updated Jul. 11, 2017 9:28PM ET
Published Jul. 15, 2013 4:45AM ET

"Zimmerman case will test tough-on-crime prosecutor Angela Corey."
Orlando Sentinel.
April 21, 2012.

What is a Special Prosecutor? – Law Offices of Thomas Ehrlich
notguiltynj.com/what-is-a-special-prosecutor

Richard Dool, George Zimmerman trial: Meet the attorneys
HLNtv.com Cable News Network, Inc.
23 June 2013

Murphy, Bridget, Shorstein dismisses longtime assistant, Florida
Times-Union 17 November 2006

Trayvon Martin special prosecutor Angela Corey is …
cbsnews.com/news/Trayvon-Martin-special-prosecutor-angela-corey-
is… Jul 12, 2013

Who Is Special Prosecutor Angela Corey? – CBS Miami
miami.cbslocal.com/2012/04/11/who-is-special-prosecutor-angela-
corey April 11, 2012

Bernie de la Rionda – IMDb imdb.com/name/nm5344026

Bernie de la Rionda, Self

Dershowitz: 'Prosecutorial Tyrant' Violated Zimmerman's …
newsmax.com/Newsfront/Dershowitz…
July 14, 2013

Prosecutor John Guy repeats obscenities during opening …
local10.com/news/2013/06/24/prosecutor…

Prosecutor (John Guy) Says George Zimmerman Shot Trayvon Martin
… reason.com/2013/06/24/prosecutor-says-zimmerman-shot-Trayvon-
m   Jun 24, 2013, ABC News.

Opening statements begin Zimmerman trial — CNN
cnn.com/2013/06/24/justice/zimmerman-trial
June 24, 2013

What the Zimmerman Prosecution Did Not Do (and Why)
americanthinker.com/articles/2013/07/…
July 19, 2013.

What the Zimmerman Prosecution Did Not Do (and Why) By Jason
Kissner. … there's more, courtesy of a post-trial, July 15 interview
with Zimmerman prosecutor John Guy.

George Zimmerman Trial: Man who shot Trayvon Martin was …
cbsnews.com/news/george-zimmerman
Jun 25, 2013

Ex-area man (Richard Mantei) prosecuted Zimmerman - The Blade
toledoblade.com/local/courts/2013/07/…

Martindale.com/jacksonville/florida/richard-w-mantei-790018-a/
Marissa Alexander Gets 20 Years For Firing Warning Shot. Huffington
Post. 11 May 2012.

Treen, Dana. Jesse Jackson visits Marissa Alexander, discusses case
with Angela Corey. jacksonville.com.

Angela Corey lashes out at critics of Marissa Alexander prosecution.
Thegrio.com. Retrieved 15 May 2012.

Dershowitz, Alan (5 June 2012). On Prosecutor Angela Corey's Rant
About My Criticism of Her. Huffington Post.

The Defense Team: Mark O'Mara and Don West

Orlando Criminal Lawyer - O'Mara Law Group omaralawgroup.com

Mark O'Mara and Zimmerman's Defense | Columbus Criminal Lawyer
koffellaw.com/…/2013/july/mark-omara-and-zimmermans-defense
July 14, 2013

Lawyer Mark O'Mara - Orlando, FL Attorney – Avvo
avvo.com/attorneys/32804-fl-mark-omara-1259969 Sepember 12, 2019

en.wikipedia.org/wiki/Mark_O%27Mara
en.wikipedia.org/wiki/Trial_of_George_Zimmerman#Defense_attorney
s

ccwsafe.com/page/Don-
West#/profiles.superlawyers.com/florida/orlando/lawyer/donald-r-
west/8da71b4b-f88f- 4c45-a512-92c7aedc11be.html

Don West Law – National Legal Defense Counsel donwestlaw.com
Dec 03, 2015

Don West - CCW Safe National | CCW Safe Weapon Liability …
ccwsafe.com/page/Don-West/www.businessinsider.com/who-is-mark-
omara-george- zimmerman-lawyer-2012-4

CHAPTER 5: THE LAWYER'S OATH

Supreme Court of Ohio Information Regarding Attorney Oath
supremecourt.ohio.gov/AttySvcs/admissions/affidavit.pdf

Oath of Admission to The Florida Bar
www-media.floridabar.org/uploads/2017/04/oath-of-admission-to-the-
florida-bar…

CHAPTER 6: SIX WOMEN ON THE JURY

usatoday.com/story/news/nation/2013/06/21/zimmerman-
jury/2444883/ Who are the six jurors in Zimmerman's trial?

All-female Zimmerman jury chosen
usatoday.com/story/news/nation/2013/06/20/zimmerman-jury-
chosen/2442513/

CHAPTER 7: THE BASIC STEPS OF A MURDER TRIAL

Ohio Rules of Criminal Procedure
supremecourt.ohio.gov/LegalResources/Rules/criminal/CriminalProcedure.
pdf

Ohio Revised Code Title (29) XXIX Crimes www.
codes.ohio.gov/orc/29

Ohio Rules of Court - Supreme Court of Ohio and the Ohio …
supremecourt.ohio.gov/LegalResources/Rules

Ohio Rules of Evidence - Supreme Court of Ohio
supremecourt.ohio.gov/LegalResources/Rules/evidence/evidence.pdf

Ohio Laws and Rules - Ohio Revised Code codes.ohio.gov

Criminal Code - By State | US Law | LII / Legal …
law.cornell.edu/wex/table_criminal_code

CHAPTER 8: MISTAKES BEFORE THE TRIAL STARTED

News About Florida's 2005 "Stand Your Ground" law
google.com/search?q=News+About+Florida%E2%80%99s+2005+%E
2%80%9CStand+Your+Ground%E 2%80%9D+law

Statutes & Constitution: View Statutes: Online Sunshine
leg.state.fl.us/statutes/index.cfm?App_mode=bing.com/videossearch?q
=florida+stand+your+ground+law&qpvt=florida+stand+your+ground+
law&FORM=VQFRML

States That Have Stand Your Ground Laws – FindLaw
criminal.findlaw.com/criminal-law-basics/states-that-have-stand-your-
ground.

Opponents Of Florida's 2005 'Stand Your Ground' Law …
thinkprogress.org/opponents-of-floridas-2005-stand-your-ground-law-
predicted…

Florida had first Stand Your Ground law, other states …
nbcnews.com/news/us-news/florida-had-first-stand-your-ground-law-
other.. July 18, 2013

What the Florida "Stand Your Ground" Law Says - NYTimes.com
nytimes.com/…/what-the-florida-stand-your-ground-law-says March
21, 2012

What does Florida's 'stand your ground' law say you can do?
ajc.com/news/national/what-does

Witness Preparation: What to Do, What Not to Do, and Best …
files.dorsey.com/files/upload/Marchese_Andrade_Litigation_News_20
13.pdf

Witness Preparation Techniques - OnDemand Webinar | Lorman …
lorman.com/training/legal/witness-preparation-techniques

Expert Witness Deposition Preparation Checklist - Training …
testifyingtraining.com/expert-witness-deposition-preparation-checklist

legal-dictionary.thefreedictionary.com/motive

Motive - Defendant, Crime, Prosecution, and Criminal …
law.jrank.org/pages/8663/Motive.html

What is MOTIVE? definition of MOTIVE (Black's Law Dictionary)
thelawdictionary.org/motive
Motive - lawbrain.com lawbrain.com/wiki/Motive

Top 5 Criminal Motives ~ LoupDargent.info
loupdargent.info/2013/01/top-5-criminal-motives.html

Motive (law) – Wikipedia en.wikipedia.org/wiki/Motive_(law)

Motive legal definition of motive
legal-dictionary.thefreedictionary.com/motive

Anatomy of a Murder by Robert Traver St. Martin's Press (1958)

To Kill a Mockingbird by Harper Lee J. B. Lippincott & Co.,
Philadelphia, PA (1960)

CHAPTER 9: LIST OF DEFENSE WITNESSES IN THE ORDER OF
TESTIFYING

In Contempt by Christopher A. Darden with Jess Walter, Graymalkin Media Los Angeles New York
(Kindle Edition 2016)

This Lawyer's Life by Johnnie L Cochran, Jr with David Fisher Thomas Dunne Books/St. Martin's Griffin 2002-10-11

O.J. Simpson acquitted – HISTORY
history.com/this-day-in-history/o-j-simpson-acquitted November 24, 2009

The Trial of O. J. Simpson - UMKC School of Law
law2.umkc.edu/faculty/projects/ftrials/Simpson/simpson.htm

How Reliable Are Witnesses to a Crime? alsolaw.com/how-reliable-are-witnesses-to-a-crime May 15, 2018

Rights of a Witness in a Criminal Case – Findlaw
blogs.findlaw.com/blotter/2018/04/rights-of-a-witness-in-a-criminal-case.html April 10, 2018

Witnesses in criminal cases – Avvo avvo.com/topics/witnesses-in-criminal-cases Sepember 06, 2017

Admitting Expert Testimony in Criminal Cases: What You …
theexpertinstitute.com/admitting-expert-testimony-criminal-cases-need-know October 19, 2017

The Best Case Law Database - Lexis Advance®
lexisnexis.com/Advance/Legal_Research
legal.thomsonreuters.com/en/products/westlaw/expert-materials Expert Witness Services & Materials on WestlawNext …
westlegaledcenter.com/program_guide/course_detail.jsf?courseId=100 007852

Webinars | Practical Law – Westlaw
content.next.westlaw.com/Webinars/PracticalLaw/Upcoming
Webinars? contextData...

Florida Evidence Code | The complete Florida Evidence Code
floridaevidencecode.com
The Florida Evidence Code was first introduced by the Florida
Legislature in 1974. It is based off of the Federal Rules of Evidence.
The code was one of the first codifications of the rules of evidence,
with at that point in time only California, New Jersey, and Kansas
having a set of evidence rules.

Florida Rules of Court Procedure – The Florida Bar
floridabar.org/rules/ctproc

Florida Rules of Criminal Procedures browardcriminalteam.com/rules

Using Convictions to Impeach under the Florida Evidence Code
ir.law.fsu.edu/cgi/viewcontent.cgi?article=2097&context=lr

Shooting of Trayvon Martin - Wikipedia
en.wikipedia.org/wiki/Shooting_of_Trayvon_Martin

Trayvon Martin - Story, Documentary & Shooting - Biography
biography.com/crime-figure/Trayvon-Martin
Born: February 05, 1995 Died: February 26, 2012

Trayvon Martin Shooting Fast Facts – CNN
cnn.com/2013/06/05/us/Trayvon-Martin-shooting-fast-facts Jun 05,
2013

Forensic Pathologist Says Trayvon Martin Was on Top of Zimmerman
usnews.com/news/newsgram/articles/2013/07/09/forensic-pathologist-
says...

The Trayvon Martin case: A timeline
theweek.com/articles/476855/Trayvon-Martin-case-timeline July 17,
2012

George Zimmerman Reenactment Tapes: Suspect Explains …
youtube.com/watch?v=lFWPQOknED0
June 21, 2012

Videos of the dummy in Zimmerman trial bing.com/videos July 10
2013

Videos of defense reenactment video in Zimmerman trial
bing.com/videos
July 2013

Judge rules Trayvon Martin texts, fight reenactment not …
clickorlando.com/news/2013/07/12/judge-rules-Trayvon-Martin-texts-
fight July 12, 2013

CHAPTER 10: HOW THEY COULD HAVE WON

How to Win Your Criminal Trial - youblawg.com
youblawg.com/criminal-defence-lawyers/how-to-win-your-criminal-
trial January 11, 2013

How to Win Trial Manual - Sixth Edition - PDF eBook
jurispub.com/How-to-Win-Trial-Manual-Sixth-Edition-PDF-
eBook.html
Ralph Adam Fine pulls no punches. In the sixth edition of his highly
acclaimed book, The How-To-Win Trial Manual, he shows why the
traditional ways to try a case in court are suicidal and gives extensive
examples of such suicidal advocacy by famous, high-profile, well-paid
trial lawyers. In each of his examples, Ralph Adam Fine shows how the
lawyers could have done a better job.

How do Criminal Defense Lawyers Win? - Colin T. Nelson
colintnelson.com/how-do-criminal-defense-lawyers-win

downtowncouncil.org website of the JAX Chamber Downtown Council
Jacksonville, Florida

Tips for the Beginning Prosecutor trialtheater.com/documents/So you
want to be a prosecutor.pdf

Winning a criminal trial based on self-defense—YouTube
youtube.com/watch?v=wsyadz5a5e8

Winning Opening Statement hccla.org/winning-opening-statement
October 19, 2014

How to Win the Trial of the Century: The Ethics of Lord Brougham
and the O.J. Simpson Defense Team Albert W. Alschuler*
chicagounbound.uchicago.edu/cgi/viewcontent.cgi?
article=1975&context=journal_articles

Intimate Partner Violence, Sexual Violence & Stalking (CDC) Bureau
of Justice Statistics, National Crime Victimization Survey
National Data on Intimate Partner Violence, Sexual Violence, and
Stalking

National Intimate Partner and Sexual Violence Survey Summary
Report (2010)

Prevalence and Characteristics of Sexual Violence, Stalking, and
Intimate Partner Violence Victimization — National Intimate Partner
and Sexual Violence Survey, United States, 2011

USA Today Yamiche Alcindor, USA TODAY Published 3:30 a.m. ET
June 21, 2013 | Updated 4:56 p.m. ET June 21, 2013
brandongaille.com/18-statistics-on-abusive-relationships/
huffpost.com/entry/domestic-violence-statistics_n_5959776, WOMEN
10/23/2014 09:25 am ET Updated December 06, 2017

cdc.gov/violenceprevention/communicationresources/infographics/info
graphic.html?

CDC_AA_refVal=https%3A%2F%2Fwww.cdc.gov%2Fviolencepreve
ntion%2Fnisvs% 2Finfographic.html

CHAPTER 11: "NOT GUILTY!"

Zimmerman Is Acquitted in Trayvon Martin Killing - The New …
nytimes.com/2013/07/14/us/george-zimmerman-verdict-Trayvon-
Martin.html

Celebrities are furious with the George Zimmerman Verdict and doing
everything to show it
businessinsider.com/george-zimmerman-verdict-celebrity-reactions-
2013-7

Atlanta News Now:
ajc.com/news/courtroom-reaction-after-zimmerman-not-guilty-
verdict/HiIhOLrMgxBrivh9n67OAL/

Ellie Hall,
buzzfeednews.com/article/ellievhall/celebrities-on-twitter-react-to-
george- zimmermans-acquittal

Andrea Mandell, Celebs react to George Zimmerman verdict
usatoday.com/story/life/people/2013/07/13/celebs-react-to-george-
zimmerman- verdit/2515113/

huffpost.com/entry/al-sharpton-Trayvon-Martin-rally_n_1370301
Corey Booker: @CoryBooker
Ja Rule: @Ruleyork Michael Moore: @MMFlint
Marlon Wayans: @MARLONLWAYANS Steve Harvey:
@IAmSteveHarvey Andy Cohen: @BravoAndy

Vision Implementer: @Tyrese Diddy: @iamdiddy
Donald Trump: @realDonaldTrump Roddy White @roddywhiteTV
Nicki Minaj: @NICKIMINAJ #GodBlessAmerica." Eliza Dushku:
@elizadushku
Ellen Page: @EllenPage

Chris Brown:@chrisbrown, #RipTrayvonMartin Sophia Bush: @sophiabush, #justiceforTrayvon Rihanna: @rihanna, #whatsjustice #pray4Martinfamily
Geraldo Rivera Still Blaming Trayvon Martin For His Own …
newshounds.us/geraldo_rivera_still_blaming
July 14, 2013

CHAPTER 12: THE JURY SPEAKS OUT

Juror B37 says George Zimmerman feared for his life in his …
nydailynews.com/news/national/george-zimmerman-called-overzealous-fbi

The George Zimmerman Juror Haunted by Trayvon Martin's …
thedailybeast.com/the-george-zimmerman…
July 24, 2017

Zimmerman trial juror: Martin played a role in his own …
youtube.com/watch?v=ZCvItOOyED0
July 17, 2013

George Zimmerman Jurors Explain Their Controversial Verdict in 'The Jury Speaks' on Oxygen, ABC News:
abcnews.go.com/US/slideshow/reactions-george-zimmerman-verdict-guilty- 19657459/image-19667886

Boxing Promoter Daman Feldman on Twitter, Damon Feldman (@hollywoodbox11)
February 8, 2014
foxsports.com/ufc/haymaker/story/george-zimmerman-vs-dmx-boxing-match- cancelled-says-promoter-020814

Dershowitz: Zimmerman prosecutor ranted against Harvard(FL) The Orlando Sentinel ^ | 6 June, 2012 | Jeff Weiner jacksonville.com/news/20180501/with-jacksonville-courtroom-days-over-tough- prosecutor-never-shied-from-death-penaltyMantei not there anymore

John Guy, 22-year prosecutor, begins circuit judgeship … jaxdailyrecord.com/article/john-guy-22-year-prosecutor-begins-circuit… January 5, 2016

CHAPTER 13: CRAZY STUFF THAT HAPPENED NEXT

Mark O'Mara quits, gives parting advice to George … deadstate.org/mark-omara-quits-gives-parting-advice-to-george-zimmerman-pay-me, September 20, 2013

Mark O'Mara to George Zimmerman: "Pay Me" - Taylor Marsh taylormarsh.com/2013/09/mark-omara-george-zimmerman-pay

George Zimmerman in Trouble Again Video - ABC News abcnews.go.com/Nightline/video/george-zimmerman-trouble-20947016 November 20, 2013

George Zimmerman charged with stalking and threatening … nydailynews.com/news/national/george-zimmerman-charged-misdemeanor May 7, 2018

George Zimmerman's Wife Files for Divorce - ABC News abcnews.go.com/US/george-zimmermans-wife-files-divorce/story?id=20171165 Sepember 5, 2013

Shiping Bao, medical examiner in Trayvon Martin case, fired cbsnews.com/news/shiping-bao-medical-examiner-in-trayvon-martin-case-fired Sepember 10, 2013

Florida Legislature Passes Bill to Strengthen Stand Your … wuft.org/news/2017/05/08/florida-legislature-passes-bill-to-strengthen…

Atlanta Black Star Judge Rules Florida's Revised Stand Your Ground
Law Unconstitutional By Tanasia Kenney. July 4, 2017

CHAPTER 14: MORE KILLINGS AND ACQUITTALS: VOTE THEM OUT!

Angela Corey kicks off re-election bid | wokv.com

Democracy N0w! August 31,2016 Florida State Attorney Who
Oversaw Trayvon Martin & Marissa Alexander Cases Is Defeated in
Primary, democracynow.org

Tanasia Kenney August 31, 2016,
atlantablackstar.com/2016/08/31/controversial- florida-prosecutor-who-
lost-zimmerman-trial-and-tried-juveniles-as-adults-loses-bid-for-re-
election/

Kim Bellware, Huffington Post 08/31/2016 09:16 am ET Updated Sep
01, 2016 One Of The Most Reviled Prosecutors In Florida Just Got
Kicked Out Of Office Prosecutor Angela Corey made a name locking
up juveniles, securing death sentences and failing to get George
Zimmerman convicted.

"Bye Anita": How Chicago's Young Black Activists Fought for
Alvarez's Loss dnainfo.com/chicago/20160316/river-north/bye-anita-
activists-celebrate-anita-alvarez- ouster-with-song-hashtag/…
March 16, 2016

Cleveland Gets Rid Of Prosecutor Who Refused To Charge…
thinkprogress.org/cleveland-gets-rid-of-prosecutor-who-refused-to-
charge-tamir-rice- shooter-b8872f28c42c/ Mar 16, 2016

US: NY Rep Dan Donovan Loses Election To Army Vet | Newspaper
africanstar.org/us-ny-rep-dan-donovan-loses-election-to-army-vet
November 7, 2018

CHAPTER 15: ADVICE TO BLACK YOUTH

Jay- Z Made a documentary about Trayvon Martin's Murder
mashable.com/article/Trayvon-Martin-story-rest-in-power/

Herstory: Three Black Organizers blacklivesmatter.com/herstory/

Biography of Emmett Till, Victim of Lynching thoughtco.com/emmett-till-biography-45213

Emmett Till — FBI fbi.gov/history/famous-cases/emmett-till

The Murder of Emmett Till | American Experience | Official ...
pbs.org/wgbh/americanexperience/features/till-timeline

CHAPTER 16: BREAKING THE LAWYERS' CODE OF SILENCE

Police killings of black men in the U.S. and what happened ...
usatoday.com/story/news/nation-now/2018/03/29/police-killings-black-men-us-and- what-happened-officers/469467002
March 29, 2018

Here's A Timeline Of Unarmed Black People Killed By Police ...
buzzfeednews.com/article/nicholasquah/heres-a-timeline-of-unarmed-black-men- killed-by-police-over...
May 1, 2015

Police killed more than 100 unarmed black people in 2015 ...
mappingpoliceviolence.org/unarmed
December 31, 2015

Police killed at least 104 unarmed black people in 2015, nearly twice
each week. (See which police departments were responsible for these
deaths) Nearly 1 in 3 black people killed by police in 2015 were
identified as unarmed, though the actual number is likely higher due to
underreporting.

New developments in police shootings of unarmed black men …
youtube.com/watch?v=k9b-0KmlY_w
March 31, 2018. New developments in police shootings of unarmed
black men CBC News … recent death in California suggests police
shot the unarmed   man from behind. … of people killed by police
officers …

POLICE KILLING OF BLACKS: Data for 2015, 2016, 2017, and …
thesocietypages.org/toolbox/police-killing-of-blacks March 1, 2018